101 Hiring Mistakes Employers Make and How to Avoid Them

Books by Richard Fein

100 Great Jobs and How to Get Them

101 Hiring Mistakes Employers Make and How to Avoid Them

101 Quick Tips for a Dynamite Resume

101 Dynamite Questions to Ask At Your Job Interview

111 Dynamite Ways to Ace Your Job Interview

Cover Letters! Cover Letters! Cover Letters!

First Job

Also in the CAREERSAVVY Series™:

Anger and Conflict in the Workplace

100 Top Internet Job Sites

Recruit and Retain the Best

The 100 Best Web Sites for HR Professionals

The Difficult Hire

Savvy Interviewing

The Savvy Resume Writer

101 Hiring Mistakes Employers Make

and

How to Avoid Them

Richard Fein

IMPACT PUBLICATIONS
Manassas Park, Virginia

Library of Congress Cataloging-in-Publication Data

Fein, Richard, 1946—
    101 hiring mistakes employers make, and how to avoid them /Richard
Fein.
      p. cm.—(Career savvy series)
   ISBN 1-57023-129-X
     1. Employee selection. 2. Employment interviewing. 3. Employees—
Recruiting. 4. Hire. I. Title: One hundred and one hiring mistakes
employers make, and how to avoid them. II. Title. III. Series.

HF5549.5.S38 F44 2000
658.3'112—dc21   99-088886

Publisher: For information on Impact Publications, including current and forthcoming publications, authors, press kits, bookstore, and submission requirements, visit Impact's Web site: *www.impactpublications.com*

Publicity/Rights: For information on publicity, author interviews, and subsidiary rights, contact the Public Relations and Marketing Department: Tel. 703/361-7300 or Fax 703/335-9486.

Sales/Distribution: Bookstore sales are handled through Impact's trade distributor: National Book Network, 15200 NBN Way, Blue Ridge Summit, PA 17214, Tel. 1-800-462-6420. All other sales and distribution inquiries should be directed to the publisher: Sales Department, IMPACT PUBLICATIONS, 9104 Manassas Dr., Suite N, Manassas Park, VA 20111-5211, Tel. 703/361-7300, Fax 703/335-9486, or *careersavvy@impactpublications.com*

Book design by Kristina Ackley
Layout by Stacy Noyes

Contents

In Honor of my Parents,
Harry and Celia,
and my Brother,
David

ACKNOWLEDGEMENTS

I would like to thank the following individuals, most of whom are human resource professionals, for sharing their insights with me concerning this book.

Kim Balkcom—Osram Sylvania
Melissa Barnes—Allegheny College
Robbin Beauchamp—Stonehill College
Steven D. Bell—Arrow International, Inc.
Penny Bresky—St. John's Health Center
Eileen Burnley—Junior Achievement, Inc.
H.W. "Buzz" Buse III—The Retired Officer's Association
Patricia Clark—Allegiant Technology
Cynthia Cobb—Baxter International
Frank Cole—Wienerschnitzel
Ann Foote—Collins, Office Depot
Beverly Cox—Glenayre
Ted Daywalt, SPHR—TAMB Associates Inc.
Carolyn Elsea, SPHR—RMT, Inc.
Corey Ericson—Nicolet Instrument Corp.
Carolin Galbraith—BDO Seidmen, LLP
Nancy Grenier—CCI Diversified
Joe Grzeika—Planning Consultants, Inc.
Eldra Rodriquez Grillman—CBS News
Michael R. Gumma—Kimberly-Clark Corp.
Diane Hardin—One Price Clothing Store
Timothy Harmon—Arkansas Best Corporation
Susan K. Hart—One to One, LLC
Kristen Holmquist—GTE Internetworking
Dennis Huebner—Vapor Corp.
Dennis James—Office of the City Attorney (San Diego, CA)

Ruth Jones—Dana F. Cole and Company
Dr. Sidney Kaz—SMW Trading
James Kineer, SPHR
Karen Kovizto—Northwest Memorial Corp.
Amy LaPlante—Harvey Industries
Fred Leh—Crown Cork & Seal Company
Kathie Leslie—Lutron Electronics
Grace Ann LoCoco—Brady Corporation
Frances MacKillop—Selective Insurance Company
Wynn Merryman—Opryland Hotel and attractions
John Micalizzi—PriceWaterhouseCoopers
Jeff Olson—Velocity Business Publishing, Inc.
Robert O'Neill—Newsday, Inc.
Debra Palmer, Lutheran Brotherhood
Florene M. Reed—Oklahoma Natural Gas
Charles Rosenberg—Topps Appliances
Carole D. Santilli—Goldenberg Rosenthal LLP
Art Sharkey—Shipley Company
Vanessa Singleton—Federal Deposit Insurance Corp.
Susan Timko—Edwards & Kelcey
Jennifer Valaitis—The Sherwin Williams Company
Tim Vibrock—Great West Life and Annuity Insurance Company
Annie Wong—Prudential

101 Hiring Mistakes Employers Make and How to Avoid Them

Introduction

This book is designed primarily for human resource professionals who want to achieve the best results at the least cost as they carry out their staffing responsibilities. In addition, small business managers and entrepreneurs will benefit from learning about the hiring process for which they may be responsible.

Most material in this book reflects interviews conducted with human resource professionals who discussed with me mistakes they had made or observed and what lessons they had learned. These HR professionals represent a variety of industries from across the United States. Some material is drawn from consultants with expertise on issues dealing with the hiring process. All interviews were conducted in the latter part of 1999.

Hiring Mistakes

We all make mistakes in both our personal and professional lives. Hopefully we can learn from those mistakes and thereby minimize their occurrence.

In the hiring context, what constitutes a mistake? For the most part, the mistakes in this book refer to:

1. Hiring a person you shouldn't have hired.
2. Not hiring a person you should and could have hired.

3. Hiring a person in such a way that a potential high performer becomes less than productive.

Often we speak about by hiring the **right person or the best person**. Theoretically, you could find all the good candidates for a particular job, rank order them and identify someone as the best. Of course, by the time you did that, the "best" candidate would no longer be available, assuming they ever were. Instead, think in terms of the right candidate as someone who is likely to do the job very well, based on your considered assessment of their skills, behaviors, and motivation as compared to the stated job requirements. In that context, there would be more than one "right" candidate, albeit some will be more right than others.

No one likes to make a hiring mistake, if for no other reason than the expense involved: recruiting, training, firing, and rehiring for the same position. The reasons for such mistakes and attendant costs include:

- **The pressure of time**. Having a hole in your staff presumably means lost productivity and placing additional workload on others. The need to hire *someone* can seem compelling.

- Failure to see the hiring process from the **perspective of potential applicants and candidates.**

- Drawing upon needlessly **narrow sources of new staff** or using sources in a sub-optimal way.

- **Flaws in the interviewing process,** including the failure to ask the right questions, listen to answers, solicit information on the candidate's concerns, and provide the candidate with a realistic understanding of what his/her work life would be with your company.

- **Flaws in interview follow-up**, including insufficient and ineffective checking of references and problematic **offer letters**.

- HR personnel and hiring managers operating under **disparate perceptions of staffing** and the hiring process.

- A misplaced **reliance on technology** as a magic bullet.

- The **intrinsic uncertainty** of any endeavor that deals with people.

- Believing that the hiring of new people is a **human resource** function *only*.

While we will discuss all of these reasons in *101 Hiring Mistakes Employers Make and How to Avoid Them*, let's begin by examining the last point first.

All Recruiting—All the Time

One fundamental hiring mistake employers make is viewing the staffing process as separate from the overall operation of the business. In other words, there is a tendency to consider recruiting as beginning when a vacancy occurs, and then tasking Human Resources to fill the position. A more productive approach is this: recruit all the time with every employee involved. Your company's name recognition and reputation are everybody's business and they influence whom you can attract and hire. Similarly, every employee is a potential source for new employees (or inversely, a potential barrier to attracting new staff). Everyone can co-operate in frequently updating job descriptions so that task doesn't begin only when someone leaves the company.

In some measure, the hiring process is caught in the tension between the implied loss of revenue when a position is unfilled and the potential cost of a bad hire. Hiring managers understandably emphasize the former while HR professionals are more attuned to the latter. To the extent that time-to-hire can be reduced, there will be less pressure to hire *someone/anyone* without taking all the appropriate steps. Finding ways to reduce **time to hire** is an underlying theme for much of this book.

In the following nine chapters, we identify mistakes employers might make and ways to avoid them. While we can never eliminate mistakes completely, we can at least understand and minimize them in the future. Indeed, if we know where the potholes are in the road, we are likely to get fewer flat tires.

Chapter 1: The Pressure of Time

Often the wrong person is hired due to a perceived need to fill a vacancy as quickly as possible. The perception has a basis in reality. It is much harder for a manager to meet his/her goals while being short staffed. The opportunity cost of sales not made, service not delivered well or research being stalled is considerable.

On the other hand, the cost of a poor hire is also considerable. A company pays a person's salary while they are coming up to speed. In addition, there are often training costs, not to mention the dollar cost of recruiting the new employee. Each hiring mistake means sub optimal production, the strong possibility of morale problems, and the cost of removing someone from the company's employ. Of course, when the bad hire is removed, the cycle of recruiting costs and start-up costs starts again.

Chapter 1 deals with ways to mitigate the pressures of time, first by not starting from scratch when a new employee is being sought, and second, by identifying a number of frequently underutilized staffing sources to assist the new staff member.

Chapter 2: Creative Recruitment Strategies

Some good staffing sources are often overlooked or poorly utilized. In this chapter, experts discuss employee referral programs, corporate alumni associations, accessing older workers and recruiting new college graduates.

Chapter 3: Don't Bend Your Hiring Procedures (but you can always improve them)

Under the pressure to hire someone, employers often bend procedures to expedite matters. These short circuits include insufficient checking of references and work history, disregarding employment test results, and yielding to internal pressures. Such actions can have negative consequences for the organization. If your hiring procedures are valid and generally effective, stick with them. You also should be open to improving your current procedures. This chapter examines possible improvements for working with internal candidates and enhancing diversity.

Chapter 4: The Interviewing Process

There are many fine books available on the mechanics of interviewing. This chapter takes a different approach and focuses on perceptual issues rather than mechanical or technical ones. For example, there is the dysfunctional tendency to hire either the clone or the opposite of the person who just left. The more effective approach is to evaluate candidates in terms of the job they will be asked to do and not in contrast to previous incumbents or other candidates.

Proper follow-through can minimize interviewing mistakes. Mistakes include not giving the candidate a realistic sense of what it's like working for your company, making it too hard to say "no" to your job offer, and a lack of courtesy.

This chapter also presents ideas on effective follow-up, including carefully considered offer letters and "after-offer" site visits.

Chapter 5: Checking References

One bane of the hiring process is the reluctance of former employers to provide references. This reluctance is quite understandable given the concern over possible litigation. Still, most HR professionals do try to garner information from references, listed by the candidate or otherwise, even if the result is simply information implied by silence. Chapter 5 presents methods some people use to gather the best information they can, including informal contacts, indirect questions and putting the burden on the candidate to insure that references are forthcoming in their responses.

Chapter 6: Technology: A Tool, not a Panacea

Many technological tools can be helpful in staffing, such as Internet databases and an employment/career page on a company's Web site. This chapter examines some of the benefits, and pitfalls, of available technology.

Chapter 7: HR and Hiring Managers

The staffing process often can be smoother and more effective when there is a good relationship between HR and hiring managers. This chapter outlines techniques for achieving such a relationship: keep hiring managers current with your recruiting efforts, supply interview questions to ask, arrive at a common understanding of terminology, and show the manager how his/her best interests are served by your recruiting process.

Chapter 8: Smooth Transition

Hiring is not really complete until the new employee is successfully absorbed. This chapter outlines mistakes, and subsequent corrections, HR professionals have made. These include preparing for potential rough spots, making the orientation meaningful instead of procedural and giving the new, eager employee a chance to hit the ground running.

Chapter 9: Obvious Mistakes, But They Still Happen

Some mistakes are so obvious we can hardly believe that they still happen – but they do. These include biased attitudes, both malevolent and subconscious, unprepared interviewers, fudging on the facts, unclear job responsibilities, lack of feedback to new employees, and assuming that the "best and the brightest" really are what the phrase implies.

Three final notes before we examine the mistakes. First, all personal and company names given in the vignette parts of this book are completely fictional. Second, since I am not a lawyer, nothing in this book should be construed as constituting legal advice. Third, because the precise point at which an "applicant" becomes a "candidate" has been a matter of considerable discussion, for clarity of presentation this book will use the term "candidate" when an applicant has been identified as a person to be interviewed for the job.

1

THE PRESSURE OF TIME

Mistakes often occur while trying to fill an open position under intense time pressures. For example, if Suzanne Jones suddenly leaves the company on Friday, her manager may want a replacement "by the following Monday." The manager's wishes are certainly understandable. Having a staffing gap makes it that much harder for the manager to meet his/her objectives. However, the very urgency of filling the vacant position increases the probability of hiring less than the best candidate. That of course means sub-optimal productivity and the potential for a turnover statistic down the line.

The following mistakes emphasize ways to minimize the pressures of time by having plans and staffing sources in place before a specific search begins.

Mistake 1: Viewing counterparts as competitors

Your counterparts in the profession can be an enormous asset, even if they work for a competitor. For example, Felicia spent a lot of time sourcing and interviewing Charlie. However, another candidate was offered the position. Felicia knew that Michelle, an HR counterpart in another company, had an open position for which Charlie would be a good fit. Felicia sent Charlie's resume to Michelle. A year later, Michelle was able to return the favor, saving Felicia's company time and the cost of an extended search.

8

LESSON: Many salespeople are used to building networks with professional and civic organizations as a way to prospect for business. Some companies are now taking a similar approach to prospect for new employees. Your professional and social contacts can be useful in sourcing job candidates and in getting informal feedback about candidates you are considering. Cooperative relationships, even with counterparts employed by competitors, can help your company. When one hand washes the other, they both get cleaner.

Mistake 2: Starting from scratch

When Samantha left for a better job, Joel was assigned to recruit for the newly vacant position. "That position is really one of a kind here," Joel thought to himself. "I guess I'll have to start from scratch."

The "from scratch" part of Joel's thinking was a costly mistake. There was already a potential pool of applicants to consider. For example, Joel could have at least reviewed the files of candidates for other positions who made the short list but weren't offered a position. Those individuals may have possessed many of the characteristics Joel needed in a good candidate and some of those people might still be looking for a new opportunity. In addition, Joel could have done a "key word" search on the database of previous applicants who weren't invited to an interview. Of course, this would require Joel's company to have a systematic way to access those files in the first case and a viable electronic database of applicants in the second.

LESSON: Yesterday's rejected applicants can still be a resource pool for tomorrow's hires. When we tell applicants that "your resume will be kept on file for six months…," we should really mean it.

Mistake 3: Not having a complete plan in place

A partial hiring plan is an asset, but you will still be losing precious time if your plan is not complete. Withit Corporation, for example, was well aware of the need to reduce the lead-time between knowing about an opening and starting the process to fill it. When Larry announced he was leaving for greener pastures, Sheila in HR was more prepared than the company had been in the past, but not quite ready enough. She had an up-to-date job description, and knew of many sources to seek a new employee. Unfortunately, she didn't really have a full-scale plan. Sheila hadn't:

- Obtained a pre-vacancy authorization to fill the vacancy should the need arise.

- Anticipated needs by staying close to chitchat and anticipating future staffing moves.

- Established benchmarks or a time line to measure progress.

- Established a recruiting budget.

- Identified potential candidates on a just in case basis

As a result, those steps took several weeks to complete.

LESSON: Especially when it comes to key employees, a complete plan for replacing him/her should be in place. An updated job description is an important first step but it doesn't constitute a complete plan. Get hiring managers to review resumes even when not looking for a new hire. Stay in touch with prospects even when nothing specific is cooking.

Mistake 4: Being reactive instead of proactive

Hiring the best candidates requires a pro-active rather than a reactive approach to staffing. Again, the key reason is the pressure of time. A proactive approach requires time *before* vacancy occurs, but lessens the time-to-hire *after* a vacany occurs. Let's compare the two approaches:

	Re-active approach	Pro-active approach
Job Description	Use the description of the person who just left.	1. Carefully consider the skills needed to achieve the goals which are ahead. 2. Update job descriptions annually, better yet quarterly.
Recruiting Process	Start from scratch	Have a base of possible candidates to contact.
Selection Process	Cut corners in the name of being expeditious	Conduct a careful screening, including the best reference check possible.

LESSON: Hiring should be an on-going process involving the total health and growth of the organization. Pro-active staffing best assures quality hiring.

Mistake 5: Interviewing candidates you wouldn't hire

It is a waste of time to interview applicants you wouldn't hire for policy or legal reasons. Therefore, it makes sense to deter them from even applying. Take, for example, the case of Growthco. As Growthco was expanding, the need for additional employees became pressing. The good news was that Growthco was able to attract a significant number of applicants for the open positions. Some of these did well in the interview process and were offered positions contingent upon passing a background check and a drug test.

The bad news is that a significant percentage of these "almost hires" failed the drug test and/or had felony conviction records. Does it really make sense to continue the interview process with individuals who couldn't be hired in any event due to legal or policy reasons? What creative things can companies do to avoid this colossal waste of time and some of the potentially adverse reactions from applicants?

Growthco decided to deter as many non-hirable applicants as possible by prominently displaying posters in the main interview area regarding criminal background checks and drug testing. In addition, applicants were asked to answer "yes" or "no" to a statement on the application form indicating they understood that a drug test would be given and a criminal background test undertaken.

"People self-selected out and reduced our lost interview time substantially," the HR manager noted with satisfaction.

Afraidtoask, Inc. had a similar problem with talented individuals who could not meet requirements for employment under the Immigration and Naturalization Act (e.g. U.S. citizenship or Permanent Resident status). One problem was that interviewers didn't want to ask about visa-status for fear of offending applicants or appearing discriminatory. However, the number of individuals who accepted offers but couldn't meet the requirements of the I-9 form forced a resolution of the issue. Afraidtoask, Inc. took the following steps:

- Since the company wouldn't sponsor for even the most highly technical positions, that fact was clearly stated in job postings of all kinds.
- A statement that the company could not sponsor under any circumstances was repeated in the letter inviting the applicant to an interview.

Ronald Rose of Rose Rix & Bennett, LLP (www.roserix.com) shares a letter from the Special Counsel for Immigration Related Unfair Employment Practices, Civil Rights Division of the U.S. Department of Justice indicating that the following set of questions is acceptable.

1. Are you legally authorized to work in the United States? __yes __no.
2. Will you now or in the future require sponsorship for employment visa status (e.g. H-1B visa status)? __yes __no.

This "set of questions seeks the information you require, without having to inquire into specific citizenship categories," the letter states. The Department of Justice continues that it does "not recommend asking applicants to specify their citizenship status in the context of the employment application process" and considers that questions "asking applicants to explain the basis of (their) employment authorization" may be too vague or confusing to them, and may not elicit the necessary information.

Afraidtoask began to ask *every* candidate the questions noted above and did so at the very first interview. The result was a sharp decrease in I-9 problems without vulnerability to legal challenges.

LESSON: Find ways to get answers to important employability questions with legal implications. Start by asking your company's legal counsel to determine what approaches to this and other legal issues you should pursue.

Mistake 6: Not using a telephone pre-screen when possible

Some HR professionals save a great deal of time by conducting a telephone pre-screen of applicants they are considering for an in-person interview. A HR person can call the potential candidates and assess enthusiasm and communication skills in a short conversation. They also can address significant issues such as geography, salary, or working conditions. The main purpose of this interview is to eliminate up-front an obviously inappropriate candidate.

If the candidate will speak with you at the time of your initial call, you may gain an added insight as to how the person handles himself/herself when they aren't expecting a specific situation to arise. Of course, if the candidate expresses a desire to speak with you at a later scheduled time, that request should be respected.

HR professionals usually close the telephone interview by doing one of the following:

- Tell the candidate that they are not the match you are looking for, then thank him/her for their time and interest.

- Thank the candidate and tell him/her that you will respond, one way or another, by a certain date.

- Arrange for an in-person interview in the case of a top choice candidate.

LESSON: Using the telephone to pre-screen candidates can save you a great deal of time and money and eliminate many potential surprises.

Mistake 7: Sourcing only those who are looking for a job

If you are sourcing only those people who are looking for a job, you are missing a large pool of potential candidates. Tight, Inc., for example, found a way to attract the so-called passive candidates. Tight, Inc. faced a very difficult labor market for the skill sets and certifications it was seeking. It tried all the reasonable approaches to attracting candidates that its competitors used, e.g. job fairs, Internet bulletin boards, advertisements, etc. The underlying difficulty was that the people Tight, Inc. wanted were in high demand so they were not prone to be looking for new employment. Such individuals are often called "passive candidates" to distinguish them from the "active" candidates who are looking for a new position

A new HR staffer, Gail, thought about her own job search process. "I built an outreach list of companies of potential interest to me. Maybe we could do something like that in reverse."

Investigating the idea, the HR staff found that relevant professional associations and journals were willing to sell membership or subscriber lists. Tight, Inc. developed a professional looking brochure that it mailed to the home address of people on these targeted lists. The brochure invited interested people to contact the firm and was accompanied by a cover letter signed by a senior manager.

Tight, Inc. found that their literature captured the attention of a significant number of potential candidates who then contacted the company. "They weren't thinking about a new job, let alone about us, until we put the bee in their bonnet," Gail noted. The senior manager who signed the cover letter was known in the field, so that attracted some attention.

LESSON: Be sure to consider recruiting "passive" candidates who require a different recruiting strategy.

Mistake 8: Assuming that passive candidates are better than active ones

Not sourcing passive candidates has a companion mistake, namely, assuming that passive candidates are necessarily better than active ones. That was the situation at Superiorco. In reviewing both interviewed candidates in general and those who became new hires, Superiorco learned a valuable lesson: The passive candidate may simply be an individual who lacks initiative or who is a marginal performer who hasn't been fired. The active candidate may have newly acquired marketable skills or be facing a change in life situation that prompts a move. "We found that the terms 'active' and 'passive' tell you nothing *a priori* about the individual," the HR Manager at Superiorco noted after carefully evaluating both types of candidates.

LESSON: Treat both "passive" and "active" candidates as equally important in the hiring process.

Mistake 9: Not updating your recruiting strategies

Niceco was reasonably successful in attracting job applicants and hiring good people. But as time went on, recruiting expenses increased and hiring success decreased. HR initially related this unwelcome combination to the tight labor market.

An HR employee began asking recent hires how they had pursued their job search prior to coming to Niceco. This feedback enabled the company to re-allocate resources to more effective channels. HR also asked the new hires what their friends were using in *their* job searches. The additional information identified avenues Niceco had not previously considered, such as using the Internet and professional network for recruitment.

LESSON: Keep up-to-date on the latest hiring strategies. After all, your competition probably is doing the same!

Mistake 10: Not sowing the seeds among the young

One way to prepare your staffing sources in advance is to reach out to potential hires before they are even old enough to be thinking about a serious job. For example, Remoteco is located in an essentially rural community, one hundred miles from any major population center. The location made it difficult to attract young singles or dual career families.

HR tested the proposition that some of the local young people would return to the area after college if they were aware of good career prospects. To that end, Remoteco began making career-based presentations in the local high schools and even the lower grades. The purpose was to put the name of Remoteco in the consciousness of local people even before they started thinking of careers. Remoteco also stepped up its summer hiring of local high school and returning college students as a means of building relationships early.

After a few years, Remoteco experienced an increase in job applicants from local people who had left for college or other reasons.

LESSON: It's never too soon to sow the seeds for recruiting future employees. Let people know your company is a great place at which to work.

Mistake 11: Ignoring the retired worker

Many companies are missing out on an experienced and potentially motivated source of employees, the retired worker. Retirees can often be accessed and attracted to your company. Jim, for example, was the honoree at a Niceco retirement dinner. "There have been fewer dinners like this," someone noted, "There aren't that many people who stay long enough to retire." "Jim looks great," said someone else, "I'm sure he's really going to enjoy golf and fishing."

Brenda was Jim's junior by twenty years, and her mind was on staffing her organization, not retirement. However, Brenda was open to new ideas. "There are retirement communities all around here. Maybe some of those folks would like to go back to work at least part-time. Maybe we should pro-actively reach out to them."

At first there was considerable reluctance to source retired people as new employees. "This is a young company, they just won't fit." "Will 30 something managers want 60 something staff?" "What about the medical costs?"

While the issue was being discussed, some younger people were hired, in part under the duress of "finding somebody in this tight market." When several of these hires turned out to be "overpriced and under-producing," Brenda's suggestion was adopted on a trial basis.

One advantage of hiring retirees is the possibility of hiring them only for the part of the year when they are most needed. Prorating a salary over, let's say three months, may lead to savings, compared with a full time salary.

LESSON: Niceco started to reach out to retired people in its area, utilizing the press in towns with substantial over age 65 populations and retiree organizations. This outreach yielded a pool of experienced people who were not prone to job-hopping. Some were able to benefit Niceco with perspectives gained while working at other companies in the industry.

Mistake 12: Forgetting the military veteran

Reaching out to military veterans is not just patriotic; it is also good business. Unfortunately, some misconceptions still stand in the way of reaching out to these people. Marty, for example, was leaving the military after ten years of service. He had risen to the rank of captain and had distinguished himself during the Gulf War. It took him six months to find a good job and Marty was wondering why.

Meanwhile, Dan, the staffing manager at Eventualco, was wondering why the ex-military candidates he was interviewing weren't passing through their interviews. Dan discovered a number of unspoken assumptions about military veterans. Since few of the existing employees had served in the armed forces, several erroneous perceptions seemed to be influencing potential hiring decisions. These included, incredibly enough:

- Officers don't have a work ethic. They just give orders.

- Enlisted personnel don't think. They just take orders.

- The people coming out of the military won't be able to relate to civilians.

- They won't be able to relate to someone younger who may be their manager

- The military is not a business, therefore ex-military don't understand profit/loss considerations.

Dan showed hiring managers how these perceptions could be negated or verified on an individual basis through the interview process. Further, even in the absence of P/L experience, the military candidate may have substantial experience in assessing value added. As a consequence of Dan's actions, his company hired Marty and broadened its effective pool of candidates.

If you are interested in sourcing US military veterans, you may wish to consider contacting a group like **Vetjobs.com** (www.Vetjobs.com), a group of professional military personnel managers.

LESSON: There are at least three dollar-saving benefits of hiring separated military personnel:

- They tend to be in good physical shape, potentially reducing costs associated with medical care and absenteeism.
- If the separating individual returns to their "home of record", the government may pay relocation expenses.
- US military veterans are a great source of talent without I-9 problems.

Mistake 13: Not utilizing career fairs to the best effect

Career Fairs can be a valuable tool for identifying good candidates. However there's more to it than just paying your registration fee and showing up. Wiserco discovered from experience that it needed to take these steps to make Career Fairs pay-off for them:

- Assess the probability that the fair will attract the people of interest to you.
- Know how and to whom the Career Fair sponsor will publicize the event.
- Staff your booth with some line managers who can speak about the relevant job openings from personal experience.
- Have an attractive backdrop and/or table covering for your booth.

- Plenty of literature about your company should be available for the taking.

- Make sure every handout includes contact information about your company.

- Encourage those who visit your booth to leave a resume and/or e-mail address.

- Make contemporaneous notes about those who visit your booth, particularly those who you would strongly wish to pursue (or strongly wish to avoid).

- Send a follow-up letter or e-mail to those who visited your booth.

- Observe what other companies are doing as a source of ideas to try (or to avoid) in the future.

- Be polite to everyone, even those who are of no professional interest to your company.

- If it is a college career fair, pens, stationery, freebies and food are useful attractions to your booth.

LESSON: A career fair can be a good hiring tool, but making it successful requires a lot more than just showing-up. There is serious work to be done, before, during and after the event.

Mistake 14: Neglecting the open house as a recruiting tool

Welcome, Inc. learned from experience how to use an "open house" event as a staffing resource. By issuing an open invitation to visit your place of work, you can achieve some or all of these benefits:

- A more controlled environment. After all it's your house and you don't have to share prospects with other companies.

- Prospects get a chance to see your lovely facilities and meet your company's wonderful people.

- If your location, facility, environment are a turn-off to some candidates it is better for them to know that early rather than have you expend major resources on the interview process.

Some thoughts to consider:

- Planning an Open House is a drain on HR time.

- Managers must participate for the event to succeed.

- HR needs to decide whether you prefer the risk of having attendees who are unqualified to the risk of missing out on good prospects. Then you can decide whether to have an utterly open door or one that opens only to a specific invitation.

Be careful in planning the hours of the open house (evening is probably better) and avoid scheduling that conflicts religious holidays or competing events (e.g. Monday Night Football).

LESSON: An Open House can be a valuable hiring tool, but the time commitment of employees, both HR and others, is considerable.

Mistake 15: Ignoring another company's downsized employees

Sometimes bad news can be good news. Although the economy as a whole has been expanding, some companies have laid off large numbers of employees as a result of mergers or a decision to downsize.

For a company looking for new employees, another company's lay-offs can be your gold mine.

It would be a mistake to believe a *priori* that the employees let go were among the bottom achievers. The company may have been motivated to eliminate the function, not the person.

The company that is downsizing is most likely eager to help its erstwhile employees. After all, unemployment compensation costs and morale of remaining employees are at stake. Therefore, contact the downsizing company to learn about outplacement agencies they are utilizing or job fairs they may be holding.

LESSON: Not pursuing downsized employees of another company may be like looking a gift horse in the mouth.

Accessing the Downsized Workers

Luke McGlynn, SPHR, Vice President of Human Resources at Secura Insurance has been on both sides of this situation. He offers these helpful suggestions:

- When you become aware of a downsizing, contact the HR Manager directly.

- You can introduce the subject by saying something like "I understand that you are going through a difficult transition. I would like to help."

- If the downsizing has not been publicly announced, but you are aware that it is brewing, make the contact anyway. However, your approach needs to be somewhat more sensitive. You might say, "I understand from some informal sources that you might be undergoing some difficult transitions…"

- Be prepared to follow through in some specific ways that are amenable to the other company. For example: Offering to conduct interviews at their site or at a hotel near the company. That minimizes lost work time for the interviewees. Alternatively, offer to do something less high profile like making the other company aware of openings in your company.

Remember this can be a winning situation for everybody. Your company could get a good employee. The other company demonstrates that it tries to take care of its workers; minimizes unemployment compensation expenses; suffers less productivity loss from worried workers. What's more, the person who was about to be out of a job knows that he or she will soon have a new one.

In Luke's view, the downsized employees you interview need to be put under the same scrutiny as other job applicants, neither more nor less. Do not assume that those caught in the downsizing were the least productive employees.

Mistake 16: Not recognizing the challenges of smaller businesses

Smaller businesses, those with no more than 500 employees, may face hiring issues that are somewhat different than larger organizations. Dr. Don B. Bradley III, President of American Marketing Group (don.bradley@conwaycorp.com) defines the issues in this manner:

- **Research:** It is more difficult for a small company to research the availability of the talent it needs, particularly if it is planning an expansion. It's not unheard of for growth plans to be short-circuited because the active labor pool just isn't accessible. Yet smaller companies are especially dependant on the labor market because they are usually in no position to use high salaries to outbid competitors for existing talent at other corporations.

- **Diversity:** Large companies realize the need to diversify the demographics of their workforce, even if social consciousness and legal considerations didn't prompt them in that direction. That understanding is often less evident in smaller companies which means that they are trying to draw on a truncated labor pool. What makes it worse is that this is a two-sided issue. Smaller businesses have more trouble attracting female and minority candidates because those groups tend not to be noticeably present in the existing workplace. It's an unfortunate Catch 22. How many white males would be attracted to a workplace that was entirely female and minority?

- **Fringe Benefits:** Many small companies have not given sufficient thought, let alone sufficient financial resources, to fringe benefits. That can be a bigger recruiting disadvantage than the (often-realistic) perception of lower salaries.

- **Continuous recruiting:** The smaller a company is, the less likely they are to engage in continuous recruiting. The volume of hiring is relatively low and other priorities are more pressing. Therefore the smaller company doesn't have the advantage of a continuous presence in the labor market.

On the other hand, smaller businesses could have a comparative advantage in some areas:

- **Care about their employees:** It is frequently the case that smaller companies care more about their employees as people, in part because the managers and/or owners are apt to see them everyday and even live in the same community. This is a great drawing card for people who have witnessed insensitive treatment at larger companies.

- **Variety and Impact:** Of necessity, smaller companies are likely to afford the opportunity for broader, more varied tasks that have a greater impact on the company. That can make the workweek more enjoyable and provides a great training ground for future entrepreneurs.

- **Training:** Larger companies are often viewed as providing better training, but that is not necessarily so. Hands-on, on the job training may be less sophisticated than classroom style training, but it is more appealing and efficacious for some people. For those considering their own business down the road, working for a small business first can be a great training ground.

Staffing For Start-Up Ventures

Start up ventures also face some staffing issues which are different from larger, more established companies, Eric Sigler, Principle at The Pacific Firm (eric@pacfirm.com) shared some thoughts on this subject.

New Venture

First of all, these are very fragile companies that have a very short window of opportunity in which to bring their new idea to market before the four other ventures in the same space beat them. As a result, they need to build entire management teams from scratch in a very short period of time.

In this time-pressed setting, cultural fit becomes less of a concern because A) early stage companies tend to not have ingrained cultures yet and B) candidates that would consider start-up companies tend to be self-selecting and have similar traits (i.e., they aren't afraid of risk, are technologically sophisticated, and understand the lifestyle and uncertainty associated with an early stage venture).

Similarly, in this environment where hundreds of new ventures are both forming and failing monthly, it has become more acceptable (or at least more of a necessity) to change jobs frequently. As such, employee retention isn't based solely on managing employee satisfaction. Instead it is driven by the harsh economics of employee stock options. Companies must continue to grow and keep employee options "in the money" and they must pile additional options onto employees so that they always have unvested shares. This is the glue that keeps employees in place. As soon as the upside is taken away, employees are much more likely to consider the numerous opportunities presented by cold-calling recruiters (some of our candidates report receiving dozens of calls PER DAY from recruiters offering new opportunities).

Candidate priorities have changed as well. In the start-up environment, candidates are less concerned with job stability, stamping an established name on their resume, or even base salary. Instead, they want to know:

- Who are the investors?
- What is the revenue model?
- What does the competition look like?
- and how many stock options can they get?

Given that new ventures seem to comprise an increasing portion of the economy, these trends will increasingly impact the broader labor market.

2

CREATIVE RECRUITMENT STRATEGIES

Several experts caution companies to better use a variety of staffing sources, such as employee referral programs, older workers, corporate alumni, and college recruits. Consider these sources seriously.

Mistake 17: Neglecting employee referral programs

Tom Darrow (TomDarrow@mindspring.com), President of HR Connections & Consulting, Inc. and an expert on Employee Referral Programs, shares his insights on the importance of such programs.

Question: Could you give a thumbnail definition of an Employee Referral Program? Also, how common are they in the United States?

Response: An Employee Referral Program is a corporate program designed to incent, recognize and reward employees who refer new hires to the company. The purpose of the program is to secure better hires and to do it better and cheaper. Many companies have a Program, but most don't do it well.

Question: **What are some of the advantages of establishing an effective Employee Referral Program?**

Response: There are at least seven benefits to the company involved:

- Low cost relative to alternate methods.

- Potential for higher caliber candidates because their skills, behaviors and cultural fit have a reliable and accessible source of reference.

- Empower employees by involving them in what is usually perceived as a management prerogative and strategic initiative.

- Increases employee morale and loyalty.

- Candidate has positive pre-disposition to company due to affinity with the referring employee and that employee's positive example and testimony.

- Candidate is contacted proactively instead of waiting for him/her to take the initiative.

- Limited competition for the candidate.

Question: **What is the first step in setting up a good Employee Referral Program?**

Response: You need to get a management buy-in. To achieve that I recommend doing a cost/benefit analysis. For example, identify your sourcing and cost metrics (e.g. cost per hire, time to fill, and quality of candidate) from the prior two years. Then estimate the cost of the program to your company. The two main components are marketing and referral bonuses. Then either calculate your break-even point (e.g. the number of hires through the ERP that would make it pay for itself) or estimate the increased number of hires.

Once you have your dollar data, anticipate other concerns management may have. For example, managers may be concerned about hiring candidates because of their relationships instead of their skills and their fit. Make sure that you have an assessment process in place that is the same for all candidates, irrespective of source. Management may also be concerned an Employee Referral Program may have an adverse impact on diversity goals. You should be prepared to show how your diversity initiatives counter any tendency in that direction.

Question: **What are some of the initial steps that need to be taken?**

Response: The company needs to make several determinations, for example:

- Who is eligible (possibilities are: management, HR, recruiting, contractors/temporaries; alumni; vendors; others.)
- What positions are eligible?
- How openings will be communicated?
- What the referral process and documentation will be?
- How and when to communicate candidate status?
- The incentives in terms of rewards and recognition?

Question: **How should the company design the referral bonus system?**

Response: First, let me say that referrals should be part of every employee's performance evaluation. After all, strengthening the company is part of everyone's job.

In terms of rewards, a company should consider cash, stock, vacation time, gifts, and tickets to exclusive events, among other things. The level of reward may vary with the position level and/or your urgency in filling it.

By the way, I would give some type of reward for every referral, even when it doesn't result in a hire. That might include some logo giveaways or chances in a company lottery, for example.

Question: **What training would you require for an employee who wants to participate in an Employee Referral Program?**

Response: We want to train employees to be effective recruiters. The six main topics I would include are:

- How and where to source/network.
- How to build relationships.
- How to assess potential candidates.
- How to sell by understanding a candidate's key decision factors.
- The importance of confidentiality.
- How to work in the corporate process.

Question: **Are there any potential negatives of which HR professionals need to be aware?**

Response: Some employees can get overly involved and start referring people from all over the place. That just generates paper. Also, some employees may make promises or reveal information that is inappropriate. These are topics you should address in your training program.

> ## Mistake 18: Not recruiting older workers

One large, underutilized source for new employees is comprised of older workers. About one-third of the American workforce, or about 45 out of 136 million, are over the age of 45. Many individuals over the age of 45, and even at younger ages, feel that they are often not welcome by prospective new employers.

Deborah Russell, Program Specialist at the American Association of Retired People (www.AARP.org), addresses several issues relevant to older workers:

Question: **Is discrimination against older workers a significant reality in their professional lives?**

Response: Yes, it certainly is. AARP continues to receive letters from members who feel they have been discriminated against based on their age. We are continually fighting in the courts and our legislatures to strengthen age discrimination laws. We have found that the problem is pervasive all across the country.

Question: **Can you identify any stereotypes regarding older workers that impede their ability to find a new job?**

Response: Two are very common. First, there is a perception that older workers are not sufficiently up-to-date with technology, for example, computers. A second is that they are inflexible and set in their ways.

Question: **Is there any legitimate basis for those negative perceptions?**

Response: In terms of technology, the perception is much less valid than it would have been a few years ago. Today, you can't really do most jobs without a functional knowledge of computers, so competency in their use is widespread even among the over 50 group. Besides, technology is in a constant state of change. Many employers find a need to upgrade the training of all their employees, not just the older ones.

Are some older workers inflexible? Of course! So are some younger workers. It is a matter of the individual, not the person's age.

Question: **In the AARP's report, "Older Americans and American Business," your survey found that HR employers also have a perception that older workers are actually superior in a number of characteristics, including commitment, working well with others, stability and loyalty. Why don't the positives outweigh or at least neutralize the perceived negatives?**

Response: Let me tell you what I think is operating here. First, there is a serious disconnect between what people recognize consciously and what they actually operate on. That disconnect can be particularly insidious when the underlying assumptions which cause it are unrecognized.

For example, many younger people have a perception of older people that they simply don't question. If they see an older person driving, they might assume that the person drives slowly or is indecisive. Or they might immediately assume that an older person is less vigorous. That younger person wouldn't consider himself or herself to have a prejudice, but in reality they do.

Also, many young people perceive an older job applicant to be their parent. What they then feel is that "I don't want to supervise my mother or father." Extending from that, a person in their 30's finds it difficult to feel comfortable with a 50 year old as a peer. Like tends to hire like, as we say, and the younger person tends to not see much likeness in the older applicant.

Question: **At what point in the job search process does this negative perception of the older worker manifest itself?**

Response: Very often it happens at the resume submission stage, particularly if the applicant has not taken steps to de-emphasize his or her age. If the applicant can get to the interview, the situation tends to improve.

Even at the interview stage, there are barriers. First, of course, are the unstated perceptions and discomfort we mentioned earlier. Second, the interviewer may actually try to disinterest the candidate in the job. For example, the interviewer may cite a lower salary or lower status, but the candidate can feel very unwelcome simply by the questions of that type that are asked.

Sometimes, even if the interview went well, the interviewer will reject the older person's candidacy on the implicit assumption that s/he is just looking for a place to roost before retirement.

Question: **Isn't it legitimate, even necessary, to probe the candidate on issues like motivation and job satisfaction?**

Response: Yes, but listen to the answers and assess the situation based on the individual, not the age. Also, the interviewer should be careful not to ask those questions in an accusatory or demeaning way. If you constantly asked an Afro-American candidate about their interest in music or athletics, there is a good chance they would draw a negative inference.

By the way, it's interesting that some companies with a high staff turnover still express a concern that the older workers plan to retire in 3-5 years. How long are they retaining their other workers?

Question: **Are there steps an employer can take to be more "older worker friendly"?**

Response: Yes, indeed. For one thing, check your help wanted ads. Do they seem to suggest that only younger people need apply? For example, I saw an ad that said the company was a "cool" place to work, and located near exciting nightlife. If you read that, wouldn't you feel that the company was sending a message of specific interest in younger people and, conversely, less interest in older people? I would even add a statement to the ads that workers of all ages (over 18) are welcome to apply, the way we make statements in regard to ethnic and gender diversity.

By the way, think seriously about putting your help wanted ads in local newspapers rather than mega-newspapers like the Washington Post. The local press is more likely read thoroughly by people over 50.

Question: **Speaking of diversity, many employers sponsor diversity training in connection with minority ethnic groups. Could employers do something like that with older people?**

Response: Yes, indeed. AARP has information on that very subject. Write to AARP Economic Security and Work Issue, Age Diversity in the Workplace, 601 E Street, NW, Washington, DC 20049.

Question: **So far, we have been seeking out older people who are still in the work force. How about the people who have entered into retirement?**

Response: Many people today view retirement as an opportunity to do or try something new. Retirement no longer means playing golf all day. Retirement has become a cyclical experience—a chance to do something different, including going back to school, starting your own business, starting a new career. Many retirees are reentering the workforce, whether full-time or part-time because they enjoy the challenge and vigor of being in the workplace.

Mistake 19: Not utilizing your corporate alumni

Some companies are utilizing corporate alumni associations as a means to attract job applicants. These associations, composed of retired and/or currently working former employees can be both a direct source of candidates and a source of referrals. Corporate alumni organizations are a relatively new but growing phenomenon.

We spoke with Glenn Kaufman, founder and president of Corporate Alumni, Inc. (www.corporatealumni.com) to learn how these organizations can be a benefit to the "alma mater" corporation and a good staffing resource.

Question: **We are all used to the idea of college alumni associations, but why are we now seeing the emergence of alumni organizations based on the relationships of former coworkers?**

Response: People spend more of their waking hours at work than anywhere else. Today's workplace is a kind of home or second family to many people. Staying connected with former colleagues serves a multitude of purposes including:

- A friendship circle of people sharing common experiences.
- A source of new employees for your new company
- A network for your own professional advancement
- A source of professional advice
- A source of personal advice.

Question: **Do alumni of a given company need permission of their "alma mater" to start this type of organization?**

Response: No. People can do that on their own.

Question: Even so, are there advantages to a company in being a sponsor?

Response: Definitely. For one thing, it helps promote an employee friendly image, which is a useful attribute in recruiting new employees. That image can also have a positive impact on potential customers and business partners.

Second, it creates an easily accessible vehicle for re-hiring so-called "boomerang" employees, folks who have left the company, whether voluntarily or not, that the company would now like to have back.

Question: Let's discuss possible reservations about business alumni associations. For example, are some people are gun shy about the boomerang employee?

Response: Yes, some companies are concerned about any lingering sense of bitterness if the employee had been let go, perhaps in a downsizing. In any individual case, of course, that should be probed in the interview process. However, remember that being invited back tends to be flattering. Also, it may simply make good business sense for the employee involved.

From the employer's perspective, the boomerang employee is going to get up to speed more quickly because s/he already knows the company and the culture. Instead of the classical honeymoon period where people are just learning about the company, you have a re-connection.

Question: Is there a risk that competitors will gain easy access to talent you developed?

Response: Yes, but competitors are already hiring and taking advantage of a company's alumni while the alma mater is not. Also, isn't it much better to have a competitor to hire your alumni than to hire away your current employees?

Question: **Will the benefits justify the costs for a company sponsoring its alumni site?**

Response: Yes. If a company works with us, for example, we design a Web site for that group's needs and we provide several Web pages that the company can use for alumni newsletters, job postings, etc. If a company gets one or two hires from its own alumni association, that alone would compensate for any financial outlays involved.

In terms of good will with your alumni, getting involved on the ground floor is the best idea. Be savvy and take the high road on this. Once an organization is up and running, corporate sponsorship is much less needed though still appreciated by alumni.

Let me add a note about possible reservations a company may have about sponsoring a corporate alumni association. Corporate alumni associations are going to be established anyway. With the Internet, people are finding it easier to stay in touch with others and to organize.

Question: **So far we haven't discussed an outside company finding employees through another company's association. How is that done and are there any ethical or legal barriers?**

Response: First, the sites are not the property of the particular alma mater company. Company X can simply contact Company Y's alumni association directly. Since we are speaking about *former* employees, Company X should have no legal or ethical objection. To clarify this, a company cannot legally gain access to the site of another company. An alumni site is reserved for its members. However, a company can place postings on the alumni site.

Mistake 20: Not doing college recruiting well

The college campus can be an excellent source of new hires, with about one million people earning a bachelor's degree each year. Unfortunately, many companies have not been as successful as they could be in utilizing this resource. Marilyn Mackes, Executive Director of NACE, the National Association of Colleges and Employers (www.jobweb.org), shares her insights on college recruitment:

- **Start with a plan:** This would include an assessment of your company's staffing needs, your comparative advantages and disadvantages based on name recognition, industry attractiveness, geography and other factors which are likely to influence forthcoming college graduates. Also know what your internal parameters are, how your company will absorb the new employee and what the potential opportunities for advancement are.

  Identify in advance which management people will be actively involved with your efforts because they are often essential to your success.

- **Targeted Selection:** Identify potential target colleges based on their fields of study, quality of graduates, demographics (including geographic base). Remember that if you don't need rocket scientists, there is no need to re-cruit at a college simply because its students are academi-cally at the top. Look at the alma mater list of your current employees and see if graduates of some colleges have worked out better for you than others.

- **Build a relationship:** Once you have identified colleges that seem to have the potential for being a good source of new hires, don't just show-up on interview day. It's impor-tant to build a relationship throughout the year and from year to year. You can do this by sponsoring speakers to clubs, financially supporting student events, providing the faculty with case studies or other materials for classroom use.

    If the college offers a co-op or internship program, that could be a good source of future employees, and a way to keep your company's name in front of students. In the short run, it can also be a good source of temporary employees.

- **The Career Office is your professional friend:** The ca-reer office staff can help you identify the best ways to position your company on that specific campus, key people to know on campus and effective ways to source the can-didates you want to attract.

- **Your counterparts can be your allies:** Your counter-parts in other companies tend to be very open to sharing ideas, best practices, etc. To access these people, get in-volved in a group like NACE or one of the regional orga-nizations.

- **Smaller companies can be players, too:** Small compa-nies can be successful, especially in your local colleges. Many students have a positive perspective about small com-panies in their area because they won't have to relocate and may not have as much away-from-home travel. A family friendly atmosphere can also be a big plus, and the opportunity to be involved in a wide spectrum of professional experiences is often a big selling point.

- **NACE can help:** NACE will be happy to help you with your college relations program. The most efficient way is through NACE membership, which provides publications, online resources, research, professional ethics, and services designed to assist you in connecting with the college campus, the college career services office, and the college student. Many NACE resources, however, are available separately as well as through membership. Three resources, in particular, that can help you build, refine, and/or enhance your college relations and recruitment program are the *NACE Directory, The Employer's Guide for College Recruiting and Hiring,* and the *Salary Survey.* The *NACE Directory* puts more than 7,900 college career services and staffing professionals at your fingertips. An excellent tool for conducting research and networking, the *Directory* provides primary contact information, plus key information about campus interview schedules, student demographics, and more, NACE's *Employer's Guide to College Recruiting and Hiring* is a "how-to" publication covering the essentials of a well-planned, well-executed college relations and recruitment program; it will help you position your program and reach your recruiting goals. NACE's *Salary Survey* gives you starting salary information for more than 70 fields of study to help you ensure you organization's compensation structure is competitive. Customized salary information is also available through NACE. In addition, NACE provides benchmark trends information, professional development information, and print and web resources for the organization interested in connecting with the college market. For more information contact NACE at 800/544-5272 or visit NACE's web site at www.jobweb.org.

3

Don't Bend Your Hiring Practices (But You Can Always Improve Them)

There are three quick messages in this chapter. If you have a hiring process that works, don't circumvent it. Be as careful with candidates you have known or who have been referred to you as you are with other candidates. Consider some new approaches to diversity.

Mistake 21: Short-circuiting the hiring process

Even if you think you know the candidate from observing his/her performance, circumventing your usual hiring process can backfire. The story of Jeremy illustrates the point. In January, Jeremy was hired at Certainco as a contract employee for six months. He was to fill an important, but not vital, role until a "permanent" person could be hired. Certainco still hadn't filled the position six months later and Jeremy's manager was pleased with his performance. "Let's offer Jeremy the job and end this endless search. He's been here for six months and done a fine job," the hiring manager said.

Shortly after being hired as a regular employee, Jeremy's performance went down hill and even his attendance became irregular. By year's end, Jeremy was fired.

Certainco had short-circuited its usual hiring process to hire Jeremy. "We figured that six months of observing his performance was sufficient," the HR manager said. "Looking back, we never really understood why a talented guy like Jeremy was working on short-term contracts." It seems that Jeremy had a pattern of being on his best behavior for limited periods of time, and then reverting to unreliability and poor performance.

"If we had probed him more about his work history, or better yet at least tried to check his references, we would have found out things we never suspected," the HR manager realized in retrospect.

Bending the system also came back to bite Niceco. That company had a numerical system for ranking candidates and a minimum passing score for each position. From time to time, a candidate was offered a position even though s/he did not obtain the minimum score. The rationale was that the numerical system was not perfect, so Niceco should be a bit flexible.

In every case, being flexible resulted in hiring a person who was pleasant and communicative but couldn't do the job.

Upon examination, Niceco realized that the numerical process evaluated technical competence and critical thinking, not just communication skills and a pleasant personality. Being "flexible" in regard to the numerical system was ended.

LESSON: Temp and contract workers can be part of your applicant pool, but don't assume that what you see short term is what you will get long term. Don't neglect usual procedures like checking references when considering them for regular employment. Also, if your hiring procedure works, don't abandon it in the name of flexibility.

Mistake 22: Overfluffing the candidate's feathers

Going out of your way to accommodate a candidate can create expectations of favorable treatment that you don't intend. The situation can be exacerbated if the candidate came to you from a well-connected source. For example, Charlene came highly recommended to Certainco by a friend of the CEO. HR set up a special videoconference interview to expedite her candidacy. Although Charlene was very impressive, HR insisted on interviewing other candidates and conducting a standard reference check. Charlene withdrew her candidacy 48 hours after her interview, citing "HR foot dragging" as her reason.

Some senior managers were upset by the loss of an apparently great candidate. However HR took the view that Charlene had saved Certainco from a potentially bad hire. Why? By the way she withdrew her candidacy, Charlene had demonstrated a lack of patience in issues dealing with her personally, a disruptive characteristic in Certainco's collegial and sometimes slow decision making culture. When the dust settled, Certainco decided not to bend its hiring procedures at all, even ruling out future videoconference interviews for high profile candidates.

LESSON: Bending your normal hiring process may lead to unrealistic expectations and subsequent ingratitude instead of a good hire.

Mistake 23: Hiring because of the connection, not the candidate

Would you marry someone because you admire his or her roommate? Hiring someone because of your connection to or high regard for another person can lead you to a similar mistake.

Jack came highly recommended by his community civic association friend, Ian. Jack was an acceptable but not outstanding candidate. The hiring manager overcame his reservations, in part because *Ian* was a great worker, who in fact had been of considerable assistance to the manager's operation.

Jack stayed with the company, establishing a performance record that was acceptable but not great. "I can't fire him, but I wish he would quit," his manager said.

LESSON: With Jack's story in mind the company amended its referral policy. Employees were reminded that an employee referral did not constitute an obligation on the company's part to hire. Managers were reminded to focus solely on the quality of the candidate and not to consider the referring source.

Jeannine echoed the story about Jack in a different way. She was referred by her sister's husband, a senior manager. The hiring manager, Louis, felt that it was a no-brainer. Jeannine had the credentials and was a pleasant person. Hiring her meant filling a position immediately, with no significant recruiting cost. Besides, maybe Louis could win a few points with someone more senior.

Unfortunately, Jeannine fell victim to animosity within the department due to what was perceived as a nepotistic hire. This occurred despite the fact that her performance was top-flight and her last name differed from that of the senior manager.

Imagine what would have happened if Jeannine had been a poor performer or had a recognizable last name!

LESSON: Recognizing the difficulties caused by Jeannine's case, the HR Manager adopted a devil's advocate approach to such hires. She reminded hiring managers that referrals of relatives or friends by employees would be subject to a higher level of scrutiny by other employees. Further, a conflict of interest might develop if the referral's sponsor and his/her manager were at odds over something.

> ## Mistake 24: Giving extra weight to well-known warts

Current employees should not be held to a higher standard than outside candidates. Larry worked at Nowco for three years when an opportunity for a better position arose in another department. "I have the skills they need and it would be a step up for me," Larry thought. He went through the entire interview process, but was not offered the position.

It seems that Larry had experienced conflicts on several occasions with some relatively senior managers. "I've seen Larry roll-up his sleeves and do a great job, but at the same time I have seen his warts," the hiring manager remarked.

Partially to protect himself, the hiring manager passed on Larry and hired an outside candidate, Herbert, instead. "If Larry blows up, my boss will wonder about my judgment, since Larry has a history in that regard. On the other hand, Herbert seems fine and his references check-out."

Herbert was satisfactory, but was he more of an asset, all things considered, than Larry would have been? "Probably not" was the consensus opinion.

LESSON: It is difficult to make a fair comparison between a candidate whose warts are visible and one whose warts haven't surfaced yet. HR worked on two fronts. One was to remind managers to probe for weaknesses of concern to them in *all* candidates. The other was to work with the internal Larry's to remove warts to the degree possible.

Hiring from within can be beneficial to your company, but it needs to be handled carefully.

Advantages:

- Boosts employee morale as more people can aspire to upward movement with the company.

- Encourages the company to train internally for the future.

- Internal posting is cheaper than external advertising.

- There are no recruiter fees or relocation expenses (of course, an inside employee who is being geographically moved is another matter).

Disadvantages:

- Peer to Manager syndrome. It can be difficult to manage former peers or to see a former peer as your manager. Of course hiring within the company but outside the immediate unit obviates that problem.

- Employees who are passed over may resent the insider more than they would an outsider.

- The employee you promote will also need to be replaced.

Mistake 25: Letting current reality stifle your efforts at diversity

Sometimes it is necessary to create a new image before it is possible to create a new reality.

Gabrielle was very conscious of the need to consider the match between candidates and organizational culture when making hire/ no hire recommendations. The culture in one unit was dominated by "40 something", married, mostly white males who believed that Monday Night Football should permeate their discussions all week. "Don't blame us. We're open to anybody with talent" was their sincere (albeit not well examined) response to a request for help in attracting a more diverse talent pool.

Gabrielle tried without success to bring in more women and ethnic minorities as job candidates. However, the (accurate) perception of the prevailing culture discouraged these very candidates.

LESSON: When it comes to diversity, it is important to break through barriers created by past experiences. In this case, Gabrielle convinced management to fund an "image advertising" campaign in minority magazines and in local college newspapers. The image to be projected was of a community conscious corporation with a commitment to diversity. The campaign apparently reduced the reluctance of minorities to apply for positions.

Mistake 26: Getting stuck in the "like referring like" syndrome

Sometimes excellent candidates come through referrals, and this tool shouldn't be neglected. The down side is that "like tend to refer like." For companies attempting to diversify their work force, a stream of such referrals may come into conflict with the diversification goal.

LESSON: Several solutions have been suggested. One was to utilize internal support groups in outreach efforts if their demographics corresponded to the diversification goal. A second was establishing ties with community groups with under represented populations. A third was increasing presence at minority job fairs and cultural events. Using a diversity of tools increases the likelihood that your pool will be diverse.

Useful Web Sites for Diversity

Ted Daywalt (President of TAMB Associates; daywalt@ mindspring.com) has identified these Web sites as being useful for diversity hires (Please remember that addresses for Web sites may change over time):

Afro-America—the Job Vault
> http://www.afroam.org

Asia-Net
> http://www.asia-net.com

Asian Jobs
> http://www.asia-net.com

Association for Women in Computing
> http://www.awc-hq.org

Black Collegian
> http://www.black-collegian.com

Black Data Processing Association Online
> http://www.bdpa.org

Career Women
> http://www.careerwomen.com

Diversilink
> http://diversilink.com

Diversity Employment
> http://www.diversityemployment.com

Diversity Search
> http://www.diversitysearch.com

Equal Opportunities Publications, Inc.
> http://www.eop.com

Feminist Career Center
> http://www.feminist.org/911/911jobs.html

Hieros Gamos (Comprehensive Law and Government Portal)

http://www.hg.org/employment.html

HispanData (National Diversity Recruitment Services)

http://www.hispanstar.com

International Career Information, Inc.

http://www.rici.com

Job Web (National Association of Colleges and Employers)

http://www.jobweb.org

LatPro Professional Network

http://www.latpro.com

Minorities Job Bank

http://www.minorities-jb.com

National Black MBA Association

http://www.nbmbaa.org

National Diversity Newspaper Job Bank

http://www.newsjobs.com

National Society of Black Engineers

http://www.nsbe.org

Net Noir

http://www.netnoir.com

Women Connect

http://findjob.womenconnect.com

Women in Technology & Industry

http://www.witi4hire.com

4

THE INTERVIEWING PROCESS

I nterviewing and hiring candidates does not always go smoothly. Several HR professionals identify dysfunctional tendencies in interviewing, the follow-up process and offer letters, along with good ways to avoid those mistakes.

Who(m) are You Hiring?

Mistake 27: Hiring the person who just left

We have all met someone like Susan, someone we like personally and respect professionally. When Susan left to take another job, her manager wanted to hire "someone just like Susan". Honoring this request opened the company to multiple hiring mistakes:

- Her manager did not articulate the traits that had made Susan successful.

- The nature of the job would need to change to meet changing needs. Had Susan stayed, she would have needed a modified skill set.

- Susan left because she felt under-utilized. Hiring her clone could be hiring a turnover statistic.

LESSON: Hire for the open position, not to replace the person who just left. Clearly articulate the needed skills and characteristics.

Mistake 28: Hiring the opposite of the person who just left

It isn't just great employees like Susan who pursue other opportunities. Steve was a disaster, according to his manager. When Steve left, the manager told HR "not to recommend another turkey like that one." The contra-indicators, as implied by the manager, included Steve's former employer, his alma mater and his specific sense of humor. To please the manager, who was adamant about his dislikes, HR recommended an objectively certifiable non-Steve, who didn't work out any better.

LESSON: Sometimes attempting to avoid one mistake leads to making another. If someone didn't work out, it is important to identify fully and accurately the cause of the failure, not simply the easily visible facts about the erstwhile employee.

Mistake 29: Evaluating someone other than the actual candidate

Sometimes it is easy to lose sight of the candidate you are actually evaluating, as the next two mistakes remind us.

At Firmco, the HR department reviewed notes interviewers made during the initial hiring process for those employees who subsequently didn't work out so well. One frequent type of comment in those notes was "he reminds me of John, or Mary", recognized stars at Firmco.

As it turned out, the points of similarity were largely external—education, appearance, social background. Of course, those attributes don't reveal anything about skill sets or motivation. Firmco found that discussions involving "the candidate reminds me of so-so", evolved into discussions of "so and so" and not the possible match between the present candidate and the job. Such discussions were banned when evaluating candidates, resulting in a more focused examination of the actual candidates.

LESSON: Analyzing the possible match between a candidate and a job is a rigorous exercise that can be undermined by surface comparisons with other people.

Mistake 30: Comparing to other candidates instead of the job requirements

At Oneco, an effort was made to identify two or three strong candidates for an open position. At that point, a group of HR people and line managers sat around a big table and evaluated the candidates and put them in rank order.

Unfortunately, the discussions often evolved into a comparison of John to Mary or Mary to James. Lost in the process was a comparison of John, Mary, and James to the requirements of the job.

LESSON: Oneco established a different protocol for evaluating candidates. Each one was compared to the needs of the job. The candidate who came closest was the first to receive an offer.

Mistake 31: Identifying the wrong problem source

Misidentifying a problem is a good way not to find a solution.

Acertainco had a turnover problem when it hired recent college graduates. "They just don't know what they really want," said the line managers. "From now on, we're going only for experienced hires."

This decision was a non-solution. Turnover was high with experienced hires also.

A new Human Resource manager was able to improve the situation by probing experienced candidates' employment histories for job-hopping behavior, and recent college graduates for motivation and expectations.

Also, since the field was in great demand, some level of turnover was inevitable. HR convinced the line manager not to stand recruiting practices on their head for no discernible benefit.

LESSON: Misidentifying the source of a problem leads to making changes that are not improvements. Also, some problems won't disappear no matter what you do. The best you can do is reduce turnover; you probably can't eliminate it. Besides, as one HR manager said, "Turnover *per se* is not necessarily worse than retaining people who really should leave."

Mistake 32: Drawing the wrong inference

In a large, multi-cultural society, it is especially important not to draw unexamined inferences from interview behavior. Ted's experience provides a case in point.

Ted was an earnest and open-minded addition to the HR staff of a mid-sized company. He was especially alert to issues of motivation in prospective candidates.

One day Ted interviewed Len for a position in Customer Service. When Len was asked about mistakes he had made and how he handled them, Len giggled.

Len's candidacy was discussed with the hiring manager, and Ted expressed his reservations about Len's seriousness of purpose. The manager hadn't picked up any disturbing signals. By probing a bit, the manager realized that Ted simply assumed that giggling indicated a frivolous attitude, which indeed it did in Ted's hometown. However, in Len's culture, people giggled when they were nervous or embarrassed. In reality, Len's giggle reflected his deep concern over his mistakes and in fact had the kind of motivation the manager was seeking.

LESSON: Unintended misperceptions are part of life. One way to minimize erroneously screening out good candidates is to identify the specific behavior that led to the interviewer's observation. Then question the conclusions you are drawing from that behavior.

Mistake 33: Getting stuck on first impressions

Stan called Mike at home to invite him to an interview. Mike was uncordial to the point of rudeness, but did arrange to come for an interview. Stan was bracing for the worst.

As it turned out, Mike was a friendly, courteous individual. He was dealing with crying children when Mike called and initially believed that Mike was a tele-marketer.

LESSON: "First impressions are not necessarily accurate impressions," as Stan concluded from this experience.

Mistake 34: Confusing incident with pattern

Towards the end of a screening interview, Steve, an HR recruiter, asked Dave to describe a time when he had a problem with a co-worker and how he handled it. Dave answered openly, honestly and extensively about a problem relationship that was not yet satisfactorily resolved.

For Steve and the hiring manager at Thatco, the story Dave related was a major red flag. There were other candidates to consider, and Dave was sent a no interest letter.

A few years later, Dave became a Thatco employee by dint of a merger. His performance reviews at the other company were excellent and Dave continued to produce in the newly merged company.

LESSON: Steve wanted to learn from an apparent mistake. In reviewing his notes, Steve realized that he had taken the story Dave told as being representative of Dave's character. "I was right to see a red flag, but I was wrong to leave it at that. I should have probed the following question, 'Was the behavior Dave demonstrated an *incident* or a *pattern?*' Apparently, it was an unusual case and shouldn't have resulted in eliminating Dave from the hiring process."

Mistake 35: Evaluating with undefined terms

When two or more people have different perceptions of the same term, reaching a decision based on uniform criteria can be difficult. For example, Wonderco arranged for Rose to interview with manager-level people after she successfully passed her initial interview with HR. Two of the managers were asked to probe Rose for evidence of assertiveness, an important characteristic for the open position. On the surface their opinions were conflicting: one regarded Rose as pleasantly assertive while the other wrote that she was not particularly assertive at all.

The hiring manager conferred with HR and decided to find out more from the other managers who interviewed Rose. As it turned out, each cited similar answers as the basis for their disparate opinion. The difference really centered on varying understandings of the term "assertiveness."

LESSON: Working with various line managers, HR developed a two-fold approach. First, HR developed a consensus definition for the key characteristics that positions required. Second, disparate opinions on generally strong candidates were probed to identify the underlying behavior. This process helped eliminate the effect of different perspectives on terminology.

Mistake 36: Confusing the quality of the interview with the quality of the candidate

Lon looked good on his resume, based on his education and experience. However the HR interviewer noted that Lon had terrible presentation skills. This comment was based on Lon's fidgeting in his chair, lack of eye contact and similar interviewing deficiencies. The hiring manager ignored HR's negative recommendation and hired Lon. Within a year Lon was a top performer in his unit.

This wasn't a case of dodging a bullet or getting lucky. The manager carefully assessed the skills she needed. "I am hiring a professional researcher, not a professional interviewee," she reasoned.

LESSON: Remember to evaluate the candidate based on the skills and characteristics needed for the job, not on his/her interviewing skill *per se*.

Mistake 37: Confusing articulate with intelligent

The opposite situation occurred with Don, who interviewed extremely well. People at Ideaco were especially impressed with his articulateness. However, Don was hired for a position that didn't require the ability to articulate as much as the ability to listen in order to glean new ideas. Don stayed on the job, but performed below the high expectations Ideaco had of him.

After Don's first annual review, the hiring manager realized that she and others at Ideaco had assumed articulateness equated with intelligence. By uncovering that unspoken, and inaccurate, assumption, Ideaco has avoided this mistake with future candidates.

LESSON: Be careful not to assume that the presence of one characteristic implies the presence of another. For example, "hardworking" doesn't necessarily mean "effective" and the ability to communicate clearly doesn't necessarily include the ability to say the appropriate thing.

Mistake 38: Poor interview mechanics

As enthusiastic as you may be about a candidate, be mindful of the following pointers to avoid making some common mistakes:

- **Don't sell too early.** You need that time to decide if you might want the candidate to buy.

- **Don't give away the answer while asking the question.** For example, if you want to probe for ability to deal with a certain type of work environment, it is better to ask the candidate to describe his/her previous working experience than to say, "It's hectic and pressure packed here, are you able to deal with that?"

- **Don't forget to take notes.** Even if you have an iron clad memory, you will need your notes to have specific reasons to support your evaluation and recommendation. Written notes are less vulnerable to the perils of selective memory and less subject to fading over a period of time.

- **Budget time to ask about all your key topics.** Make sure that you are mindful of your time so you can ask and probe on the important characteristics you are seeking.

- **Ask the candidate if s/he has any questions to ask you.** It is a simple courtesy that helps make the interview a two way street. You have been *asking* questions, why not reciprocate? The candidate's questions may indicate if s/he has any reservations or concerns that need to be probed and/or addressed. The *quality* of the candidate's questions may give you useful information, pro or con, to evaluate him/her.

LESSON: Good interview mechanics are an important part of a successful interview process.

Mistake 39: Being negligent instead of neutral about reality

It is sometimes difficult but often necessary to deal openly with a problematic reality, as this story about Lauren and her first employer demonstrates.

Lauren was a top graduate of a fine engineering program in the Midwest. She was offered a position in a manufacturing plant not far from the college. There had been some concerns whether a single woman, raised in Chicago, would adjust to small town life. "Don't worry, I spent four years in this area and loved it," she said. Since the hiring manager wanted to hire Lauren, that answer was accepted as realistic without further probing.

Lauren's initial performance was excellent, fueled by high energy and long workdays. Unfortunately, her work quality declined after a few months. A rural town of 25,000 people, mostly married, is not really like a rural college of 15,000, mostly youngish, single people.

Lauren's social life was approaching zero and that hurt her work life as well. Within a year, Lauren left for a job near a big city.

LESSON: Now, when this company interviews recent college grads, the area's social demographics are presented with neutral reality. On the upside, what social life there is for young singles is also made visible to young applicants. The candidate may start thinking about the issues more than s/he had previously and/or may reveal information that will be useful in determining if an offer should be extended.

Demographics and social reality are also important to experienced candidates. The facts about school options, housing costs and dual-career opportunities should be presented with neutral reality.

Mistake 40: Relying on untested assumptions

Untested assumptions can come back to bite you. For example, Marcus interviewed at Possibleco, a company in the same industry as his current employer. Everyone liked Marcus, who was indeed pleasant, intelligent and hardworking. Unfortunately, no one probed Marcus about his understanding of the industry, a key requirement for the position at Possibleco and a major reason Marcus' resume had gone to the top of the pile in the first place. As it turned out, Marcus was a functional expert in getting things done within Formerco, but was insulated from broader issues of the industry. Therefore his learning curve at Possibleco was much steeper than anticipated and his direct reports were often uncomfortable with Marcus' relative lack of industry knowledge. The net result was a well-intentioned, under-performing manager.

LESSON: Don't assume that a history in a specific industry equates with knowledge of that industry. "It's something we should have probed' the HR manager said. "We might ask the questions in a different way, but they still need to be asked." Another assumption that often comes to grief is that the candidate possesses technical skills based on a college degree or work experience.

Mistake 41: Accepting nice words as shared values

Sometimes we are prone to believing nice words simply because it is so nice to hear them, as some managers at Niceco learned to their regret.

Niceco is a medium sized company in its field. It's middle and senior managers had been with Niceco for an average of eleven years. They felt committed to the Niceco style of business, were proud of its accomplishments and determined to maintain a family-friendly work life. Entry level candidates often cited those very same points when asked why they wanted to work at Niceco.

Unfortunately, many of these excited candidates became dissatisfied as employees. In their exit interviews they tended to cite a desire for better pay and a larger employer as reasons for leaving.

Reviewing their entry level hiring process, Niceco found that both HR and line managers believed candidates who expressed a preference for a medium or small company and a willingness to accept lower compensation. Since these were operative attitudes for the long-term staff, the interviewers were comfortable hearing what they themselves believed.

LESSON: Don't assume that your values are the actual values of the candidate, even if the candidate says all the right things. Many candidates are not sure about their priorities and/or may simply say what they believe you wanted to hear.

Mistake 42: Rejecting a good candidate in a "plus" size

Sometimes a company passes on a good candidate due to biases that are perhaps unrecognized. Susan's story provides an example.

Susan was a bright, articulate, thoughtful candidate who didn't get hired by Firstco. Instead, she became a top manager at Anotherco, a Firstco competitor. We deliberately left out a fact that goes far to explain this outcome: Susan was significantly overweight.

The Firstco hiring manager, Dan subsequently met Susan at a conference and was impressed by her presentation relating to increased contributions to the bottom line from her unit. Dan went back and checked the notes interviewers had written about Susan. "Lacks high energy needed for the position" was noted by several people. When asked if anyone could recall why Susan was viewed as lacking energy, no concrete examples were forthcoming. However, when people referred to Susan as "that heavy woman", Dan began to sense that overweight and lazy were being equated, at least in regard to this woman.

LESSON: In a combined effort with HR, Dan encouraged people to identify their unstated biases. The result was that biased thoughts, once recognized, became less of a factor at interviews. Instead, those interviewing probed for characteristics, rather than assuming that the candidate did or did not have them.

There are certainly other biases to be recognized and challenged. For example, short men lack assertiveness and tall men are natural leaders.

Mistake 43: Ignoring red flags

Be careful not to ignore red flags under the pressure of closing a vacancy with a hire. In the next two items, we will identify some of the red flags employers may ignore to their sorrow.

John interviewed for a relatively low-level position in a manufacturing environment. He was well spoken and polite. John was more articulate than most people holding that type of position and was especially well dressed. His home address was an apartment in an upscale neighborhood.

Those who interviewed John asked why he would want a job that didn't pay all that well. John answered to the effect that he was looking for an opportunity to work where he felt fulfilled and starting salary wasn't a big issue. People liked John and accepted his answer at face value.

Within a year, John was arrested, charged with being a drug dealer. According to the indictment, John had built a network of drug users within the company and used his new job to facilitate distribution.

LESSON: Red flags don't necessarily indicate a problem with the candidate, but they do point to areas that need probing and clarification. In this case, the company realized that the apparent incongruities between John and what was more typical in candidates should have led to additional investigation. They might have uncovered the fact that John had lost his previous job for dishonesty, rather than as a result of a more general downsizing.

Mistake 44: Red flags from real life

Here's a compilation of other "red flags" that HR professionals shared with me. It would be a mistake to ignore any of them.

- Each of the candidate's past employers is out of business and no supervisors are available to comment on the candidate's work history. Similarly: Every past supervisor being retired…

- Past employers listed are entirely fictional (uncovered by calling the Chamber of Commerce to verify a business at a distant location)

- Previous job was quit without notice

- Claims that the termination from their previous job was unjustified because they won the unemployment claim

- Applying for a job that is a "step down" in terms of authority and/or pay

- Desperately needs a job—with repeated calls and visits, pleading for the position

- Consistent pattern of short tenure in past jobs

- The reason for leaving a job was a "personal reason"— especially when it is the reason for leaving **every** job

- Brings others to the interview (Especially deep shade of red: spouses who looked like they hadn't bathed in a month; a candidate brought her nine-year-old granddaughter into the interview, and a candidate who brought her baby— and her mother—to watch the baby)

- Being late for the interview without a compelling reason

- Not listening to the interviewer's questions. (The candidate that could hold the interview without you)

- Reveals too much personal history (divorce, etc.)

- Incorrect telephone numbers on the application

- Person listed as a reference does not even know that the applicant is looking for a new job.

- Looking for a job after spending only a few months on the old job. Also interviewing in another city during the work week

- Frequent (more than once or twice) career interruptions by self-employment periods

- Too much talk about employment laws (like discrimination)

- Salary given as a reason for changing jobs

- Badmouthing his previous employer/supervisor
  For example:

  > The company had management problems

  > Others favored in promotion

  > I'm not progressing as fast as I could

- References won't speak-up for the candidate

- No references listed

- Impossible to contact references

- No direct supervisors listed as references

- Income inconsistent with title

LESSON: On the road to making a good hire, there are many signs of potential problems that should prompt you to be extra careful.

Employment Applications

Some companies require a completed job application form prior to an interview. Here are two classic application form mistakes to avoid.

Mistake 45: Ignoring the answers you asked for

Steve indicated that he was a convicted felon on his application, but was not questioned about it at his interview. Steve was hired, lapsed into some unsavory activities, and had to be fired. Upon researching the matter, the company found that no one had bothered to read Steve's application.

LESSON: The simplest thing in the world is to read the application. Use it as a serious source of information and potential red flags. After all, you ask those questions for a legitimate reason. There is a second lesson: As a by-product of this experience, the company designed its application to minimize interviewing people with clear knockout factors. Specifically, the company's application stated prominently that job offers would be contingent on passing a drug test and that criminal conviction records would be examined. Subsequent to this change, fewer people with convictions completed the application process and the number of people failing the drug test dropped significantly. The company attributed these cost-saving changes to the deterrent effect of the revised application.

Mistake 46: Accepting "see attached resume"

Stephanie was asked to complete a job application. "May I just attach my resume?" she asked. "It's such a waste to repeat the same things." The HR clerk agreed. The HR interviewer, however, said to Stephanie, "Actually, we need you to complete the first part of the application and attach your resume for the other sections." Stephanie included her name and address on the application form and attached her resume.

So where is the mistake? Stephanie had written a deceptive resume to cover the fact that she had been fired twice in the last several years. Attaching her resume kept her lies consistent. Stephanie passed the interview and was hired. Within weeks she was fired (again) for lateness and for pilfering supplies.

LESSON: If the applicant can't attach their resume, any inconsistencies are more likely to surface on the application. Some companies ask the applicant for his/her resume, as well as the application form.

A more humorous mistake of this type occurred at another company that we will call Oneco. The company asked applicants to give the dates of their military service, if any. John indicated service in the navy. As it turned out, John had served in *another country's* navy, prior to immigrating to the US and becoming a citizen.

Oneco was about to embark for the first time on seeking Pentagon contracts and thought that having more US military veterans on its staff would help. John had answered the question honestly, but Oneco didn't get the veteran's benefit it anticipated.

LESSON: Make sure your employment application is explicit, clear and complete in the information it seeks. In this case, the request should have been for service dates in the *United States* military.

Following Up

> **Mistake 47:** Confusing "deciding in haste" with "hastening to decide"

Sometimes we need to take the folk song about Clementine to heart. The sorrowful protagonist lost his true love "for a courtin' too slow". Annette certainly seemed to be the perfect candidate. Her credentials were superb, her references checked out, and each person who interviewed her felt Annette was the thoughtful, flexible, collegial person the job needed.

But one line manager was hesitant. He had only interviewed three candidates, of whom Annette was the first. Fearful of being accused of hiring the first person he met, the manager insisted on seeing at least three more candidates. By the time that process was complete, Annette had accepted another position.

LESSON: If you have the right candidate and have followed your usual process in regard to that person, the number of people you have interviewed should not preclude extending an offer.

> **Mistake 48:** Over-courting the candidate

Niceco wanted to hire Jane in the worst way. To Niceco's sorrow, they did hire her *in the worst way*.

Jane had a wonderful education and all the skills her new job would demand. Niceco treated her like Cinderella, taking her out to a great lunch in an expensive restaurant and putting her up in a five-star hotel.

The problem came when the recruiting ended and the job started. Jane felt that if she was good enough for fancy restaurants and first-class hotels, she shouldn't have to do work she didn't enjoy. After six months of dissatisfaction, she quit.

LESSON: Make sure that the recruiting process includes a realistic look at the pragmatics of doing the job. If possible, have the candidate spend a day observing the unit where s/he would be working. Also, make sure your recruiting process doesn't go overboard and inflate the candidate's sense of self-worth beyond the reasonable.

Mistake 49: Making it hard for the candidate to end the process

Sometimes candidates find it difficult to end the interview process on their own initiative. "They were so nice to me and I told them I was really interested. Now I feel obligated to accept their invitation to the next interview step." This feeling among applicants is not universal but it isn't rare either.

LESSON: Some HR Professionals put the ball in the candidate's court. After stating something encouraging, they invite the applicant to call the company if s/he is interested in the next step. That saves the uninterested applicant from the awkwardness of rejecting an invitation and saves the company interview time. Otherwise the unfortunate result can be a needless expenditure of interviewing resources.

Mistake 50: Making it hard for the candidate to say "no"

Sometimes the true success of a recruiting effort depends on the candidate's rejecting the job offer.

Jack had all of the characteristics Interviewco was seeking. The company offered him a position and he accepted.

Unfortunately, Jack didn't really feel comfortable with the company's operating style, in this case a highly unstructured environment. Jack kept his reservations to himself for fear of jeopardizing the job offer. Interviewco didn't probe the issue for fear of losing Jack.

Within a year, Jack was gone.

On the one hand, Interviewco didn't want to emphasize potential mismatches between the company and the candidate. Why scare away your recruits? On the other hand, ignoring mismatches simply defers everyone's grief. What should you do?

LESSON: Some interviewers try to find a balance by asking questions about the candidate's work style preferences. At a minimum, this approach raises the issue without explicitly labeling it as a potential problem relative to the company's actual work situation.

An additional approach is to invite the candidate to spend a day observing his/her future work area *after an offer has been made*. This way the candidate is not under the stress of selling themselves and can experience the company's environment more clearly. Further, they may feel free to ask questions they had withheld until the offer was given.

Mistake 51: The interview process wasn't linked to reality

A situation somewhat similar to Jack's arose at Fantastotech. This company wanted to be on the cutting edge in its field and it hired very bright engineers. They were shown the types of projects the company was pursuing and the resources that would be available to them. Duly impressed, the engineers accepted Fantastotech's job offers. Many of them quit within a year.

The HR staff interviewed long term staff and discovered that the newly hired couldn't deal with the company's project review process. It seems that the company subjected new ideas to intense questioning and challenge by other engineers. Those who were used to being considered techno-gurus couldn't adapt to the grilling. Confused and demoralized, they quit.

As a part of the interview process, Fantastotech now has each candidate present a proposal, which is than challenged by a panel of other engineers. That way, candidates know what they will be walking into if they accept a job offer.

LESSON: Encouraging the candidate to experience a realistic slice of work life at your company even before s/he has an offer in hand can save everybody considerable grief.

Mistake 52: Attracting the candidate with a transient factor

While a positive relationship between the candidate and the company culture is desirable, a strong tie to a specific individual may not be. For example, at Funco, a top prospect chose that company over a competing offer largely because she held such a high opinion of the manager who interviewed her. When that manager left for a division on the opposite coast, the new hire lost an important reason for being at Funco and her performance ceased meeting expectations.

LESSON: Although you want to put your best foot forward and have the candidate meet with winning personalities, the ties that bind should be built *to the company* rather than to a specific individual.

Mistake 53: Neglecting courtesy

Noelle's story demonstrates how a lack of basic courtesy can have a negative impact on your business. Noelle interviewed for a highly competitive position at Couldhavebeennice, Inc. She had to sacrifice two days to attend her interviews and commuted several hours round trip each time.

Then she heard nothing. After waiting several weeks, Noelle called HR to inquire about her status. She received no response, even after she made three more calls spaced at ten-day intervals.

Six months later, HR called Noelle, indicating that her resume had been kept on file. Would Noelle be interested in interviewing for a recently opened position? Not wishing to repeat her ill treatment of half a year prior, Noelle politely declined.

LESSON: Common courtesy, if nothing else, tells us to respond to job candidates in a timely manner. Good business practice should reinforce that principle. The rude treatment experienced by Noelle resulted in a smaller potential applicant pool for Couldhavebeennice, Inc. (Minus one for Noelle, possibly minus more for people who heard her story).

Reject in a Professional Manner

Harlow Keith (HKEITH8019@aol.com) of the Keith Group suggests a rejection letter like the following:

Rejection Letter

(Name of Applicant)
(Mailing Address)
(Date)

Dear (Mr./Ms.) (Last Name of Applicant)

Hiring decisions are never easy to make, particularly when there are so many qualified applicants for an open position. Your credentials were given every consideration, but we have decided to offer the position of (Job Title of Open Position) to another person.

We will keep your application and paperwork on file for the next (indicate time period). During that time, whenever a position becomes available for which you are qualified your credentials will be reviewed. If there is an interest, we will contact you. If after (time period indicated above) you have not heard from us, and you are still interested in seeking employment with (Name of Company), please feel free to come in and fill out another application with us.

Thank you again for the time you spent with us. Your interest in (Name of Company) is greatly appreciated.

Sincerely,

Thomas Smith

Thomas Smith
Vice President-Human Resources

Offer Letters

Offer letters share little in common with creative writing. It's important to say exactly what you mean and avoid the temptation, as one HR manager put it, "to get warm and fuzzy in writing."

Mistake 54: Not being careful in what you say and how you say it

Wanda's offer letter from Warmco indicated an annualized salary, cited her potential for growth, and expressed a hope that she would remain with Warmco for many years.

Far from fulfilling those dreams, Wanda seriously under-performed and was fired within six months. She sued, claiming that the offer letter constituted a contract which Warmco then violated by dismissing her in less than one year.

LESSON: Warmco's offer letters now indicate salary in bi-weekly terms, mention the company's "hope to grow with you" and explicitly state that employment is not guaranteed. This approach removed problems like Wanda's. However, it opened Warmco to a different difficulty.

Warmco was based in an "at will" state. That is, employers could fire employees for any reason or no reason at all. The company stated their "at will" policy in their offer letter in a matter-of-fact way.

Good intentions went awry in two ways. First and worst, some individuals felt the statement suggested that the job being offered with one hand might be yanked away with the other. Second, one person accepted a job offer and quit after a week. His rational was that if employment is "at will", there was nothing wrong with quitting for any reason or no reason at all, at any time at all.

LESSON: Warmco made an additional revision to its offer letter, indicating a hope that things would work out well, that candidate and company would grow together. This tone was welcoming without making any firm commitments about continued employment.

Mistake 55: Confusing cold with business-like

Hiring is a very human process and must take into account the potential new employee's heart as well as their head.

Coldco was very eager to hire Jeannette and indeed offered her a position. Jeannette had several offers to weigh, and turned down Coldco. When the HR manager called to ask why, Jeannette said, "the offer letter was so cold, I just didn't feel really welcomed."

LESSON: Coldco now has the hiring manager call people who have been offered a position and deliver an oral "warm and fuzzy" without implying anything that could be problematic later. The manager also explains that the offer letter may seem cold but the company is welcoming.

Mistake 56: Not knowing the elements of a good offer letter

HR consultant Harlow Keith (HKEITH@aol.com) suggests these elements for a good offer letter:

- Title of the position
- Department of which the position is a part
- Pay (specified by payroll period, not annualized)
- Probationary review terms and dates, if applicable
- Reference to first and subsequent annual reviews

- Date, time, and place to report

- Anything new employee needs to bring with him or her

- A notation that a copy of the letter is being given to the person to whom the candidate will report and to *that* person's manager as well (e.g.: cc: John Jones, Manager; Sally Smith, Vice President).

LESSON: Have a checklist indicating specific points you want your letter to cover, and a sample letter to use as a reference.

Mistake 57: Forgetting that friends and family can be your allies (or your enemies)

At Certainco, the HR manager, Dahlia, wanted to know why good candidates rejected what seemed like good offers. What Dahlia found was that some candidates were putting considerable weight on advice from others, including people who had never heard of Certainco.

To minimize such loses, Dahlia asked serious candidates if they would like information about Certainco to be sent to anyone else. She made it clear that this question was not a recruiting technique to find more applicants, but rather a way to provide information to people of importance to the candidate.

The result was that Dahlia knew who the "significant others" would be in the decision process and was able to frame questions to elicit any concerns the candidate thought these people might have. Further, the information packet itself seemed to have a positive influence on the significant others.

LESSON: The candidate may not be the only one who will have a say in the candidate's final decision on your job offer. Therefore, be open to bringing those significant others into the decision process as your allies.

Offer Letter

(Name of Candidate)
(Mailing Address)
(Date)

Dear (Mr./Ms.) (Last Name of Candidate)

We are pleased to offer you the position of (Job Title of Offered Position) in the (Division/Department) of (Name of Company). Your starting date will be (Starting Date).

You will be paid $____ per (hour if non-exempt; pay period if exempt). Your probationary employment period will be for (indicate the length of the company probationary period in actual calendar days; e.g. three months=90 days), and you will be given a probationary performance view at the end of this period. Your anniversary date with (Name of Company) is (anniversary of hire date), at which time you will be given a performance review and your performance will than be reviewed annually thereafter.

As mentioned earlier, you will start on (Starting Date), and you are to report to the Human Resources Department located at (Street Address) by (indicate the starting time) on that day. Please have with you your Driver's License, Social Security Card, and all other official forms of identification so that we may complete the processing of your paperwork. Please call the Human Resources Department at (Telephone Number of Human Resources), if you have any questions.

On behalf of (Name of Company), we welcome you to our organization. We hope that your relationship with (Name of Company) will be a rewarding experience for both you and the company.

Sincerely,

Samantha Cutridge

Samantha Cutridge,
Director of Human Resources
cc: Immediate Supervisor
cc: Manager to whom the Immediate Supervisor Reports

Mistake 58: Not knowing about a possible non-competition clause

John seemed like an excellent hire. He had a solid education and impressive work experience. Indeed, for the past several years he had worked for Formerco, a company in an industry related to that of his new employer, Newco.

The first month was a great success. John was assigned to a critical project and was doing a wonderful job. Then the roof fell in. John's new company, Newco, received a letter from the General Counsel of Formerco complaining that John was in possession of proprietary secrets and his new employment was a violation of the "non-competition" clause in John's contract.

Newco faced a legal problem from Formerco if they continued John's employment and a possible suit from John if he were to be dismissed.

LESSON: Subsequent to this experience, Newco asked relevant applicants to provide a copy of the text of their non-competition clause at their current company. Responses like "It won't be a problem" or "I'm like a free agent" were no longer accepted at face value.

Mistake 59: Low-balling the candidate

Jim, in HR was under considerable pressure to prove that his recruiting function didn't rely on offering above average salaries to hire new employees. Jolene, a top prospect, seemed deeply interested in the job and perhaps a bit under the gun due to a downsizing in progress at her current employer, combined with a tenuous family situation.

Hoping to hire a good candidate on the cheap, Jim offered Jolene a low-end rather than mid-range salary. Jolene sensed that the offer was substandard and apparently related that fact to her potentially vulnerable situation. Insulted, she rejected the offer.

As a consequence, the interview process had to continue and the hiring manager became increasingly impatient. The next good candidate was offered an above mid-level salary in hope of clinching the deal. The net result was that compensation and recruiting costs were higher and needed projects were neglected for an even longer period of time.

LESSON: Don't take a candidate's enthusiasm or vulnerable situation as an opportunity to save your compensation line dollars. Your company's bottom line may suffer in other ways.

5

CHECKING REFERENCES

One thing most HR professionals agree on is the desirability of checking references. However many companies have a policy that prohibits providing any information other than job title and dates of employment. Even so, the vignettes that follow stress two main points. First, not checking references can lead to disaster. Second, when you hit an informational brick wall, find some way over or around that obstacle.

Mistake 60: Ignoring informal contacts

John was new to Metropolis when he started at the HR department of Hisco. When he tried to gain information from his HR counterparts regarding potential hires, the only information he received was dates of employment and job title.

After becoming actively involved in his local human resource organization, John found his counterparts more forthcoming, albeit in an oblique way. When John called the HR people who knew and trusted him in regard to a potential hire, the response was in code. For example, if candidate X had been a problematic employee at the other company, their HR representative would say "call me at my mother-in-law's about that." This response sent up a red flag that encouraged John to probe more extensively into the candidate's work history.

LESSON: Your contacts through professional associations are often willing to provide an informal warning about a potentially bad hire. Building those contacts and reciprocating when possible can give you the "heads-up" you need to avoid a bad hire.

Mistake 61: Not finding a wedge in the wall of silence

The reluctance of people to give references is understandable. "I call other people for reference checks all the time. However, if some one asked me to respond to my own questions, I wouldn't, because it's against our company policy to say anything whatsoever," one HR manager told me. Nevertheless, the effort must be made and sometimes it will be successful.

Dahlia found that some line managers would speak freely, perhaps being unmindful of company policy. "If nothing else, I ask one pregnant question 'Would you hire this person again?' Anything other than an affirmative answer waves a red flag for me." Shelly found that if the line manager didn't want to talk, it was helpful to keep talking anyway. Using shoptalk as a medium seemed to be helpful. Prolonging the conversation in a pleasant way enabled the line manager to convey a feeling about the prospective hire, even if s/he didn't articulate it. Whatever Shelly inferred wasn't definitive, of course, but it did provide indications of how to proceed.

LESSON: There are ways to induce some people to give you valuable information about a candidate, even if their company policy states that they shouldn't. Although no approach is guaranteed to work all the time, it is often worth the effort to ask.

Mistake 62: Being reluctant to scratch a raw nerve

Debra tried to use the "keep 'em talking approach," but was not always successful in obtaining the information she needed. She discovered one way to get useful responses was to feed back to the former manager what the candidate had told her. For example, "You must have been sorry to see James leave since he was one of your best managers and was responsible for turning around your division's P/L statement." If James had been less than truthful in discussing his accomplishments, the line manager often got emotional and let loose with information s/he felt was necessary to set the record straight.

LESSON: Asking a manager to validate information provided by the candidate may cause the manager's desire to set the record straight to overcome his/her reluctance to talk to you at all.

Mistake 63: Not getting performance evaluations from the candidate

Sheila tried the methods used by her counterparts, but was concerned that she might be drawing an inappropriate inference. To guard against that possibility, Sheila asked the candidate to provide copies of his/her performance evaluations, with any proprietary information blackened-out. An advantage of this source of information was that it was easier to ask clarifying questions of the candidate, since Sheila didn't have to protect the identity of her sources.

Larry also put some of the burden on the prospective hires. He made access to useful references a requirement for employment. As a result, candidates were more likely to ask former managers, co-workers, etc. to be co-operative.

LESSON: Place some of the burden of a meaningful reference check on the applicant.

> **Mistake 64:** Calling when you actually anticipate that someone will answer the phone

Usually, we hope that someone will answer when we place a telephone call. However, making a reference check may be an exception.

At Oneco, the HR manager, Eli, found a different way to get at least a general response from listed references. Eli called the reference at an hour when he anticipated the phone wouldn't be answered. Then Eli left this message on the answering machine, "Your name was given to us as a reference by (so and so). Please call me back if the candidate was excellent." If the reference did return the call, Eli took that as a positive sign in itself. If there was no return call, the implication was negative. "The system is not fool-proof, but it worked as well as anything else for me," Eli said.

LESSON: Leaving the next step up to the reference himself/herself may provide some needed feedback, if only by implication. Of course, it is important to realize that a non-response is not necessarily a negative response.

> **Mistake 65:** Not knowing about possible negative feedback in advance

It is certainly a live possibility that you will receive negative information during a reference check. If you are prepared for some of the specific problems, you are less likely to err by accepting such statements at face value.

This is what Oneco did when it received negative information. "The feedback put us on our guard, but negative feedback doesn't necessarily mean the candidate wouldn't work out well for us." As a safeguard, HR began to ask serious candidates "What am I likely to hear when I speak to your references?" Very often, candidates would reveal potentially negative information, but this enabled HR to hear the candidate's side of the story in advance. The candidate's information helped HR probe the reference better to see what bearing any negative comments should have on their own evaluation of the candidate.

LESSON: Being prepared for possible negative information helps you probe and assess its significance for your organization's needs.

Mistake 66: Not comparing different versions of the same events

---

Sometimes the best approach is to ask about events, rather than about the candidate. That was the approach Lucia took in trying to verify certain claims made by James, one of her candidates. After indicating that James had given the manager's name as a reference, Lucia asked about how certain things were accomplished. For example, "Without revealing anything proprietary, could you tell me about how your division met its roll-out deadlines on the 'Writopener' in 1997?" Lucia then compared the response with what the candidate had said about the "Writopener" roll-out during his interview.

LESSON: One way to get around policies that prohibit giving references is to ask about something that may be in the realm of the permissible.

Mistake 67: Forgetting to get additional names from each contact

One good way to leverage your reference checking time is to ask each reference for the names of other people with whom to speak. Claire did this with great success. In her case, she was particularly interested in friends and co-workers, for two reasons. First, they would feel less constrained about discussing the candidate. Second, given the team work imperative in Beth's company, the perspective of peers was especially important.

Even without actually getting a response from a reference, you can use that name to good advantage. You could ask at an interview, "I see that you have indicated Pat Person as a reference. What would Pat say about you?"

LESSON: Use your reference calls to widen the scope of people you can contact.

Mistake 68: Forgetting that temps are still employees

Temporary employees are still employees, as Herco, Inc., forgot to its regret.

Herco, Inc. experienced a predictable seasonality to their workflow. For real, but temporary needs, they hired temporary employees.

Unfortunately, they emphasized "temporary" rather than "employee" in their thinking. Under the press of time, Herco hired Arnie without doing a thorough background check. Arnie was available because he had trouble keeping a job. Not only was he unreliable, he was a womanizer when he did come to work. The result was the Arnie did not do what he was hired for, and he negatively impacted on the productivity of the other employees. Luckily, in this case no sexual harassment charges were brought against Herco.

LESSON: A temporary employee still needs to be screened carefully.

Mistake 69: Waiting until you buy the cart to check out the horse

Sometimes the desire to speed up the hiring process becomes a case of paying the price later instead of paying it now.

At Certainco, the standard procedure was to extend job offers, contingent upon successful completion of a background check. Unfortunately, the vendor doing the checks wasn't given any names until after the offer was made. Since the need for new employees was pressing, many people started to work before their background check was completed.

Selma had been on the job for six weeks before Certainco learned that she had lied about her education. Selma was dismissed for falsifying information, but Certainco had lost six weeks of its training investment and had to recruit for the position again.

LESSON: Certainco decided to start background checks earlier in the process. There was an extra expense up front, since not everyone would be offered a position and some would not accept the position if offered. However, for Certainco, the added expense of the background check was less than the cost of wasted training.

Mistake 70: Neglecting less formal references

There are some less formal reference sources who might be helpful in better assessing a candidate. Here are some sources that have been used to good purpose:

- Customers

- Suppliers and other vendors

- Members of candidate's professional associations

- Subordinates and co-workers

- Your professional counterparts

- The candidate's professional counterparts

Of course, these sources may be reluctant to be completely open with you, for fear of jeopardizing their existing relationship with your candidate. Nevertheless, asking the right questions can still elicit information you need. For example, rather than asking "Do you think John has good communications skills?" ask, "In what way has John exhibited his communication skills when he is working with you?"

LESSON: Think broadly about the people who are in a position to give you feedback about a candidate.

Mistake 71: Ignoring the information you get

Don't yield to the temptation of ignoring the information you acquire in a reference check simply because you are feeling good about the candidate.

Bob seemed like a swell fellow and maybe he was. Unfortunately, he was quite lax in paying his bills. Nice guys make mistakes, so interviewers didn't press the issue, which had been uncovered in a background check.

Two years later, Bob was dismissed for violating company ethics regarding purchasing contracts. Bob was struggling with a serious gambling habit. To feed his gambling fever, he accepted personal payments from vendors, misled others, and may have embezzled.

LESSON: After Bob's malfeasance was uncovered, interviewers began probing more intensively into performance history when credit problems were uncovered. As a result, several otherwise appealing candidates were screened out for prior performance problems that would otherwise have not been revealed.

Note: According to a survey conducted by the Society for Human Resource Management (SHRM), most employers have "not experienced legal difficulties resulting from references provided to other organizations or prospective employers in recent years. Only 1 percent of respondents said that defamation claims have been brought against their organizations as a result of references provided about former employees, and only 1 percent said their organization had been sued for negligent hiring for hiring individuals who later harmed another employee or committed another crime while an employee."

It is *fear of being sued* rather than the experience of being sued that prompts the tight limitations companies place on providing information about current or past employees.

Mistake 72: Not distinguishing between a reference check and a job offer

---

Make sure your candidate understands that a reference check does not mean that a job offer is forthcoming, let alone that an offer has been extended.

Herman interviewed with Infowizards and sensed that the process was going pretty well. His optimism increased when Debra, the HR person in charge of filling that position, told Herman that she was starting to check his references.

Delighted, Herman became less guarded at work about plans to leave. People began to sense that Herman was on his way to bigger and better things.

When Infowizards subsequently did not offer him a position, Herman felt bitter and even misled.

A year later, Herman went to work for one of Infowizards customers. Still nursing his wounds, however unfairly, Herman subtly wreaked vengeance by making Infowizard sales and operations staff miserable when they called on his new company.

At Itwasugly, Inc., individuals were offered positions contingent on a successful background check and drug test. Several people gave notice to their then current employer, but failed at least one contingent factor. The result was people who now had no job—an unpleasant situation for everyone involved. The company now stresses to candidates, orally and in writing, not to give notice to the current employer until clearance is achieved.

LESSON: A job candidate can be very talented in their chosen field and surprisingly unsophisticated about conducting a job search. Debra could have avoided offending Herman and the subsequent hostile relationship by clearly indicating that a reference check was by no means the equivalent of extending a job offer.

Mistake 73: Not separating the functions

It is natural, but dangerous, to screen out information which may undermine the "successful" conclusion of a search. Here is an example and a possible solution.

Sam was the lead HR person designated to recruit a new project manager. Working long hours on a difficult assignment, Sam was able to bring in Nancy, who was offered the position. Sam was praised for his good work and set to work checking Nancy's references.

The reference check should have signaled Sam to be cautious. However, even with his misgivings, Sam raised no yellow light and Nancy was hired.

LESSON: When Nancy didn't work out, the process was reviewed. The HR manager felt that Sam had screened out negative information in order to conclude the search "successfully". Viewing this as a human frailty, rather than misfeasance, the HR manager changed the system. A separate individual, with no personal stake in the candidate search, was assigned to do reference checks. This separation permitted a greater degree of independence in the reference check.

Mistake 74: Closing a position too soon

What do you say to candidates to whom you are not offering the position while you are checking the references of the applicant you selected?

One company decided in all fairness to inform the unsuccessful candidates that the position was now closed once their offer was accepted. That was a nice thought but a bad idea. The successful candidate's offer was contingent on a successful background check, which he failed. When the company then turned to the other candidates, they quite understandably expressed a diminished sense of interest.

LESSON: Answer inquiries by saying simply that the search is still in progress and that all candidates will be advised when it is complete.

6

TECHNOLOGY

I s technology a magic bullet? Not really, but it can be a useful resource. We have deliberately avoided mentioning specific vendors or products because these will change over time. Instead, we have focused on more broadly applicable principles.

> **Mistake 75:** Forgetting familiar tools that make new technology work for you

At Newtoweb, Inc. the HR Manager, Judy, was concerned about the relatively sparse response to the careers section of the company's Web site. After attending a conference, Judy tried an additional approach. She paid a relatively modest fee for the right to explore an Internet resume database. The exploration yielded more usable resumes than Newtoweb, Inc.'s own Web site.

The process worked so well for Judy that she went mining for Internet resumes as a source for important positions even before they became vacant. To offset concerns about stale resumes, Judy sent e-mail, complete with job designation, to her electronic file of plausible candidates when a position opened. Those who responded were presumed to be interested and therefore not stale.

LESSON: Judy combined a second, easily utilized resource, in this case e-mail, to minimize the shortcomings of another

93

resource, namely the potential staleness of Internet database resumes.

Mistake 76: Taking the new tool just as you find it

At Erehwon, Inc., the main Web site made it difficult to find out where the company was located. For many purposes, this was no problem because "our customers need to know about our products, not our geography." However, real people need to work in a real place, not cyberspace.

HR wanted to reduce the number of resumes submitted through the Web site by applicants with an insurmountable geographic barrier. Drawing an analogy to a simple paper form the HR manager had used at a different company, a short prescreening application was added to the Web site. It asked the applicant if s/he knew that the company was located in lovely Niceville, a town of 30,000 in northwest Wonderful State. Subsequently, the number of geographically inappropriate electronic resume submissions was reduced.

LESSON: Technology can provide wonderful tools, but human creativity and judgment are still needed.

Mistake 77: Not correcting the common flaws of company Web sites

---

Mark Hurst, President of Creative Good and Dr. Jakob Nielsen, Principal, the Nielsen Norman Group have identified a number of common flaws in company Web sites as they relate to e-recruiting.

- Company specific jargon that prospective applicants didn't understand

- Requiring a browser "plug-in" before any application could be downloaded

- Requiring registration and login before job listings could be browsed

- Users halted by error messages

- Company's location(s) not clearly specified

- Search function neither prominently visible nor easy to use

- The site's "personality" didn't match the corporate culture. Therefore an opportunity to attract appropriate applicants and deter inappropriate applicants was lost

- Unclear job titles

- Applicants slowed down by unnecessary graphics

LESSON: Tools provided by technology, e.g. your company's Web site, need to be user-friendly *for your intended users* in both the operational and perceptual sense of the term.

Mistake 78: Thinking that the Internet is a magic bullet

The Internet can be a useful tool, but it is not a magic bullet. At Quickfix, Inc., a "career opportunities link" to the company's main Web site was developed. "All our openings are now posted for the world to see" a senior manager declared. "That should save us a bundle on recruiting costs."

Of course, the fact that something is "posted for the world to see" doesn't mean that anyone will look at it. Most people don't wake up in the morning determined to checkout the specific Web site of your company. Part of the solution for that is to be linked to other Web sites, especially ones with high traffic. Prominent career bulletin boards are an example. However, those linkages do cost money and hardly guarantee results:

- People who aren't actively looking for a new job are not likely to be spending time searching career bulletin boards. Yet this is a population you want to attract.

- Your company's Web site is probably not designed with the primary purpose of attracting job applicants. Instead, it is most likely designed to promote your company's products and services. Therefore, the tone of the Web site may not coincide with the initial impression you want to convey to potential applicants.

LESSON: The Internet is not a quick fix. However, a "Career Opportunities" page can be an asset, especially if it is specifically designed to attract the job applicants you want and is easily accessible from your first Web site page.

Recruiting is still a person to person process. Electronic means such as the Internet are sourcing tools, i.e. they can help you access prospective candidates. The follow-up steps like identifying prospects, interviewing, selling the candidate on your job offer, must still be carried out well by human beings for your company to win the hires you want.

Mistake 79: Not being prepared to make adjustments

Technology can be an asset, but it can also be a two-edged sword. Oneco is a company that hires mainly technical people, like engineers. Their challenge was attracting a sufficient number of applicants. Oneco subscribed to several Internet resume-posting services, and did access a very large number of resumes.

At first, this new abundance was a problem, because Oneco was not used to reviewing large numbers of resumes. In fact, the sheer volume of resumes made review and selection of candidates slower than before. However, with the purchase of a reasonably priced software package, Oneco was able to auto-select based on a refined set of criteria it established.

"It wasn't perfect, but it was much better than what we had before. At least we could pull out the kinds of engineers we wanted and only those with some experiences who lived in places which wouldn't present a major relocation problem. We were able to source people to an extent which had previously not been impossible."

LESSON: Be prepared to make adjustments if some of the consequences of the new technology are less than desirable.

Mistake 80: Confusing new with better

In some situations, the learning curve can be costly and a new technology can be more of a burden than an asset in some cases.

At Adifferentico, the increased volume of resumes from Internet services became a burden. The company was receiving 300 resumes per day. This seemed wonderful until the HR staff realized that they didn't have readily definable sorting criteria to shape the resume mountain into a manageable hill. Adifferentico hired people with virtually any college degree and was seeking soft skills combined with high motivation. The solution used at Oneco was therefore not a good fit.

To complicate matters, many of the resumes that came in electronic format needed to be 'cleaned-up' before they could be entered into Adifferentico's database. The result was a drain on staff time.

LESSON: The cutting edge can become the bleeding edge if the proffered solution doesn't address your problem or creates more of a burden than it relieves.

Mistake 81: Not being in control of the technology

If the new technology is not within your control, you may be buying into trouble. For example, Largeco paid an outside vendor to develop a Web site for the corporation. One link was "Careers at Largeco," which included a page of descriptions of jobs currently open and information about applying.

HR was happy to have an additional means of eliciting resumes especially for its highly technical positions. A problem developed when jobs were filled in reality, but still open according to the careers link. Largeco continued to receive resume submissions for closed positions, and felt honor bound to respond to each one. This was time consuming for HR and confusing to applicants who continued to see a position on Largeco's Web site even after receiving a letter that it was closed. To the vendor, however, it was a minor glitch in an otherwise excellent Web site and they were in no hurry to fix it. Senior managers considered the matter a nuisance, not a real problem, so there was no high-level pressure exerted on the vendor.

LESSON: Technology can impose burdens if it is not under your control. A very clear statement regarding the vendor's obligation if performance is not up to HR specifications is a partial solution.

Mistake 82: Not tracking results

Some companies make another mistake with technology: they forget to establish ways to determine if certain technological "advances" are earning their keep. For example, Greatideaco paid considerable sums to be hot linked to addresses of Web sites that the kind of people it wanted to attract were likely to visit. However, Greatideaco did not put into place ways to identify which electronically submitted resumes came from a direct visit and how many came from a hot link.

LESSON: If you want to know which technologies are effective for you, establish some method of identifying results, perhaps with tracking tags. For example, put distinct job identification numbers on posted jobs. In that way, your resume count by source should be relatively easy. Alternatively, have responses from each contracted Web site routed to a distinct collection point.

Mistake 83: Not establishing criteria for evaluation

Jeannine was in her first recruiting rotation at Customer Service, Inc. She returned from a conference, excited about the success some of the small companies experienced when instituted an IVR (Interactive Voice Response) System. Jeannine convinced her manager to support trying an IVR at Customer Service, Inc. in an attempt to make hiring the annual group of customer service representatives and inside salespeople more cost effective. A toll free number for the company's IVR was included in the appropriate print media help wanted ads. Interested people called the number and responded "yes" or "no" to a series of screening questions, using a touch phone. Individuals who passed this test were invited to schedule themselves for an in-person interview. On the surface, this system saved HR a good deal of processing time. In addition, the 24/7 availability of the system seemed to attract more contact from job seekers.

The downside was a high no-show rate for in-person interviews. Jeannine calculated the cost of the IVR itself, imputed a cost of no-shows in excess of previous experience and concluded that for her company, the costs outweighed the anticipated savings. Wendy, the HR manager, decided to retain the IVR for an additional year to determine if ways could be found to make the system more effective.

LESSON: There are several lessons here. One is that what works at another company may not work at yours. A second is that another company's criteria for evaluating a system may not match yours. Third, you must determine what time frame to establish for the new system to prove its worth.

Mistake 84: Poorly designed Internet ads

It can be a mistake to retain old work styles while incorporating new technology. For example, some employers write Internet Position Openings as though they were newspaper classifieds. However, space constraints are much looser on the Internet—you are not paying by the square inch. It is especially important however to include your important "key words" so that your posting can be more readily accessed by appropriate candidates.

LESSON: Write a fully detailed job description, including necessary skill sets, years of experience, formal training, and the location of the work site. Let potential applicants know exactly what you want them to submit and how you want the material submitted. For example, should a resume be submitted by template, email, fax, or hard copy.

Mistake 85: Soliciting email resumes the wrong way

Here are some ways to avoid mistakes in soliciting e-mail resumes:

- Clearly indicate the qualifications you are seeking. Simply stating a job title and location is insufficient to either attract the right candidates or expect inappropriate candidates to eliminate themselves.

- Tell the applicant precisely how you want the resume sent. The variety of possibilities confronting a potential applicant is considerable. Do you want:

  - A Word attachment?
  - Scanable text attachment?
  - Resume posted onto e-mail?
  - Faxed copy only?
  - Hard copy only?

Some companies ask the applicant to answer a few questions via template in addition to submitting a resume. If you need *three years experience* with computer program X, why not ask, "How many years of experience with Computer Program X do you have?"

LESSON: Let potential applicants know exactly what you want them to submit and how you want the material submitted.

Mistake 86: Not knowing what makes an Internet recruiting system both effective and efficient

Christina Wilkinson, National Internet Recruitment Lead at Raytheon Systems Company, plays an important role in building a centralized

Internet recruiting system for her company. Christina shared some insights from her experience in this area.

"In evaluating commercial Internet recruiting resources, I look for a system that is both effective and efficient. To evaluate prospective sites, I use these criteria:

- Traffic and audience data. Specifically I am looking for unique visitors rather than the amorphous term "hits".

- Attention span, namely how much time is being spent on each visit.

- Number and quality of links bringing a prospective employee to that Internet site. Quality is based on links likely to be accessed by my target market. The professional associations of interest to people with the skill sets we need would be an example.

- Can the vendor provide audience data by profession/geography? This data should be available from their resume database.

- The availability of Web site statistics reporting information that allows ongoing analysis of our success, e.g., the number of impressions for each posting (how many times a job came up in a candidate's search), number of "stick-throughs" (how many searches result in someone clicking open our job postings) and the number of resume submissions for each posting.

- Is the Internet site well funded and does it have an advertising program in place?

- Affiliates. For example, are there some large boards that may be powering the smaller sites?

- How efficient is their resume search mechanism from a recruiter's point of view?

"There is no standard media matrix for Internet sites. Also, there is no outside audit to provide information. Therefore, any data you receive should not be taken at face value. Instead, utilize HR forums, news groups and experiences of your own recruiters as an important assessment tool. In addition, I always test out the site myself as though I were applying for a job. That's a good test of user friendliness.

"In terms of cost, price is often negotiable. If possible, request a free trial period or a short (e.g. three-month) contract before getting locked in for a full year commitment. Since customer service can be an area of disappointment, probe this issue as much as possible in advance.

"Internet recruiting is one of our most important sources of candidates, along with our employment Web site (www.rayjobs.com) and our employee referral program. Having our own site offers the advantage of obtaining demographic information immediately through a quick registration process and enables us to send out an acknowledgment immediately. Our goal is to shift more of our marketing efforts from job postings on career boards to campaigns designed to drive candidates directly to our employment Web site."

LESSON: If you are prepared to ask the right questions and insist on the performance criteria of importance to you, your Internet recruiting system can be both efficient and effective.

7

HR and Hiring Managers

The relationship between HR and hiring managers is not always smooth. Many admit there's room for improvement. Several common mistakes and constructive steps for hiring success are presented in this chapter.

> **Mistake 87:** Leaving the hiring manager without questions to ask

Understandably, hiring managers may not be thoroughly conversant or comfortable with changes in interviewing methods. For example, Certainco adopted behavioral based interviewing as the only approach permitted, whether the interviewer was from HR or a line manager. This is not unusual.

Barry, a line manager, had learned to prepare questions based on the candidate's resume. The new policy was to ask a pre-determined set of questions prepared by HR. "I shouldn't prepare my own questions if I'm limited to those HR gives me," Barry assumed.

After several interview experiences under the behavioral protocol, which he deemed unsatisfactory, Barry raised the matter with HR. "That's great that you are used to preparing questions, Barry," the HR manager said. "Under this system you can use the questions you prepared to help you probe the candidate's responses."

LESSON: Hiring managers may be understandably cautious when there are changes in the hiring process. HR should try to identify concerns that may not be explicitly stated. In this case, HR was able to clarify the situation and told Barry that preparing questions based on the candidate's resume is still a useful tool. The best place to use that preparation, however, may be for probing, rather than presenting, questions.

At Niceco, Jeannine was highly regarded by everyone, not least her manager, Ralph. So what's problematic about that? It seems that Ralph respected Jeannine's judgment implicitly, so much so that he never really asked probing any of the candidates Jeannine wanted to hire. The hiring process was losing the perspective and insights Ralph could have added.

LESSON: The HR Manager provided Ralph with questions to ask, based on issues important to the job and to the future needs of the company. Ralph's better questions saved him from at least one bad hire and made a favorable impression on one sought-after candidate.

Mistake 88: Not making sure that a new idea is properly understood

Explaining a new process doesn't guarantee that it will be understood. The message may need to be modified, even if the content isn't. For example, at Limited Budget, Inc., the recruiting budget was very tight. Examining where the money was spent. The HR manager identified the cost of bringing in short–list candidates to the home office for on-site interviews. "It's costing us a fortune in transportation, hotels and high level interviewing time. Let's try just bringing in two candidates at a time."

On the surface, the new system did save money. For the next search, only two finalists were brought in. Choosing between those two, "Jones," was hired.

The downside showed itself later. Despite the HR manager's (clear, he thought) statement that *neither* candidate *need* be hired, that indeed the search could go on, line managers still felt they were being asked to pick one of the two. Months later, when "Jones" didn't turn out as well as expected, this flaw in the hiring process was identified. Thereafter candidates were identified *as among the first* for whom final interviews could be scheduled.

LESSON: HR made special efforts to assure that all participants in the hiring process understood that there was no hidden agenda and that hiring policies really were as stated. These efforts included brief face-to-face meetings and material written in a friendly question and answer format. These meetings also enabled HR to anticipate future misunderstandings and address them up front.

Mistake 89: Not finding a common language

There is a lot to be said for involving people with different perspectives and areas of expertise in a hiring decision. However, it is important to establish mutual respect and some level of common understanding. For example, Kate from HR and Nate, a hiring manager, were working on filling an important position. Kate, proud of her skills in psychology, seemed concerned only about "soft skills." Nate focused on technical requirements. This division of responsibility can work, but didn't.

First, Nate lost confidence in Kate because "she only understands the 'touchy, feely' stuff." Kate felt that Nate's focus on the technical made him a bit narrow in his perspective. The consequence was a divisive, rather than complementary, search process.

LESSON: Reviewing the process, which resulted in a good hire but some bad feelings, Kate and Nate made a fundamental decision. Kate learned more about business considerations and Nate attended a seminar on staffing. The outcome was a Kate/Nate team strengthened by mutual respect, gained in part because they understood the validity of each other's language.

Mistake 90: Not demonstrating with facts and figures

If you want to gain support for a new idea, demonstrate its value with hard facts, don't simply make recommendations based on your feelings. A case in point is Streamline, Inc. HR and the line managers all realized that the pressure of hiring without long delays was leading to some questionable hires. As a result, a decision was made to streamline the hiring process by having many of the important pieces in place before a position came open.

The first step was to make sure that everybody's job description was updated annually. This eliminated some of the time spent scrambling to write a job description in connection to a new search. The second step was to have a plan in place detailing what steps would be taken, especially in regard to filling key vacancies. The third step was for both HR and line managers to be active in professional associations, making connections for possible future sourcing.

The key to gaining a management buy-in was demonstrating that the up front investment of managers' time paid dividends in quicker and better hires. This required hard numbers based on past experience, rather than philosophic generalities.

LESSON: Good ideas are more likely to be adopted if HR has the objective data to demonstrate their value to hiring managers.

Mistake 91: Leaving the hiring manager out of the firing process

---

Getting the hiring manager involved the *firing* process is a good way to drive home the importance of making a good hire in the first place. The situation at Advanco provides an example. The company had a hiring procedure that worked reasonably well. The HR people and the hiring managers got along famously and most individuals hired worked out well.

Still, the HR manager wanted to reduce bad hires as much as possible. He showed the managers the cost of a bad hire, including training time wasted and tension within the team while the bad hire is in place. In addition, there was the lost business, etc., while trying to get rid of the bad hire without being vulnerable to a costly lawsuit.

However the HR manager realized that the separation process was the sole province of HR, removing the time cost and psychological pain from line managers.

LESSON: Advanco agreed on a procedure for having the hiring manager participate directly in the *firing* process as well, including the painful aspect of breaking the bad news. The result was that managers became more cautious in hiring decisions because of the time and unpleasantness involved with removing a bad hire.

Mistake 92: Not keeping the hiring manager posted

"Do they want miracles? These things take time," Tim muttered half out loud. Two hiring managers were pressing Tim to recommend candidates to fill vacancies. Tim did the reasonable thing and sought an answer to his own question. By informal inquiry he found that the hiring managers assumed Tim was dragging his feet.

From that point forward, Tim made a point of keeping each hiring manager completely informed about efforts to fill their vacancies. It wasn't just a matter of poking in his head to say, "good morning, I'm working on it." Tim provided frequent reports of his efforts to attract a good pool, the results of pre-screening interviews, and similar developments. When the hiring managers realized the extent of efforts to fill their vacancies, pressure to complete the hire prematurely eased considerably.

LESSON: When the hiring manager knows what you are doing to staff his/her area, s/he is less likely to think that you are doing nothing.

Mistake 93: Forgetting the broader company perspective

What's good for a specific, immediate situation may not be good for the company as a whole in the longer run. Paul, who was just perfect for an open job at Newco, provides a case in point. The hiring manager wanted Paul ASAP and couldn't understand the reservations of the interviewer from HR.

Paul was hired and did a wonderful job. Unfortunately, his skill set did not position him well for a promotion or lateral move within the company. Paul started to stagnate. His performance declined but he stayed with Newco. "With no promotional incentive and with not much new to learn, Paul doesn't provide a good model for our new hires and doesn't provide the company with bench strength," the hiring manager aptly noted.

LESSON: The HR department and line managers initiated a discussion culminating in a fundamental change. Instead of hiring for the position only, as in the case of Paul, the company added the criterion of the longer-term, broader interest of the company as a whole.

An additional outcome was an articulated policy on the value of building a strong bench especially in regard to the more important positions in the company. The availability of a strong bench alleviated much of the time pressure and recruiting expenses Newco had experienced with making key hires.

Mistake 94: Giving the hiring manager more than s/he wants

More is not necessarily better, as the following story illustrates. Barry was very thorough in searching for candidates. He tracked all of the data, including number and source of all applicants, dates of any phone conversations and who initiated them, etc. When it came time for Lynn, a line manager, to interview, Barry gave her a folder that included the applicant's record of communications with the company.

Lynn wasn't pleased. She felt obligated to read the whole file prior to the interview, but wasn't really interested in anything but the candidate's resume.

LESSON: Give the interviewing managers just what they need to conduct their interview unless they request more.

Mistake 95: Forgetting that nobody is talented at everything

We wouldn't expect Mark McGuire to be good at pitching or to enjoy tennis simply because he is a great hitter in baseball. We can draw an analogy to hiring managers, as Lisa's story shows us.

Lisa felt some dread. She was in charge of filling an open position and the hiring manager, Ben, had a history of hating the whole staffing process. He hated interviewing candidates, in part because "we can't do it the way we used to."

Reviewing some office records, she noted that Ben had some history of hires that didn't work out. Otherwise, Ben was a super manager and was himself a leading candidate for promotion.

Meeting with Ben, Lisa realized that he was great at what he did but felt uncomfortable with interviewing. In addition to getting her best fix on the opening, Lisa also invited Ben to an interviewing workshop.

Ben was grateful. He had been so concerned about asking illegal questions that he didn't probe very much at all. In the past Ben had taken only the most cursory notes, which didn't really fit the needs of the hiring process. As a result of Lisa's workshop, Ralph developed better interview techniques and understood the rationale for a process he had previously scorned.

LESSON: Be a resource to your managers so they can add excellent interviewing ability to their portfolio of contributions to the company.

Mistake 96: Being vulnerable to making important decisions under duress

It is important to develop policies for difficult situations that don't allow much time for deep consideration at the time they occur. A good example is what Linda experienced as blackmail.

Andy walked into the office of Linda, the HR Director, with an envelope in his hand. "This is my resignation" he said, "Another company has offered me $10,000 more. I just can't turn down the extra money."

Linda knew that Herco was already short of programmers and was approaching a delivery deadline. Andy's manager was distraught at the thought of losing a key player, especially at a critical time. After conferring with senior managers, Linda made Andy a counter offer by the end of the week.

Linda met with key managers to decide what to do in future situations. The managers agreed with Linda that the counter offer was a bad idea. Despite Andy's importance to the company, going outside their regular compensation guidelines encouraged other employees to try the same ploy. Further, the managers agreed with Linda that even Andy wouldn't remain content with his new salary for long.

Shortly thereafter, Lon walked into Linda's office with an envelope containing his resignation. "Lon, if you will be happier somewhere else, I think you should go there," Linda said. Lon did leave the company, but visits to Linda's office with resignation in hand dropped off considerably.

"We let Andy blackmail us," Linda said. "Blackmail begets more blackmail, so we decided to stick to our salary guidelines even if it meant losing people."

LESSON: The "Andy incident" highlighted the need for Linda and hiring managers to cooperate in anticipating what might arise and to develop an agreed upon policy. That way, fewer key decisions had to be made under duress and tight time constraints. Another company might develop a different policy on the specifics of an Andy-type incident, but that policy should be developed with sufficient time to consider its consequences.

Mistake 97: Not treating the hiring manager as your customer

Doug Pelino, Vice President, Human Resource Operations and Consulting, at Xerox shared some of his perspectives on the relationship between Human Resources and hiring managers.

Question: Can you discuss some of the perceptual differences between HR function and hiring managers?

Response: An occasional difference in perception could be the immediate need versus the long-term implications of filling an open position.

Hiring managers must confront the reality of one or more vacancies in their business area. That means that work has to be redistributed or simply not done. The consequence could be the loss of revenue, reduced customer service or similar problems. The hiring manager has goals to meet and is going to be held accountable. Therefore, the manager understandably wants to have his/her openings filled immediately. On occasion, the HR function could be seen as bureaucratic, as being more concerned with process than results, and may even be viewed as a barrier to getting the job filled quickly.

Although anxious to support the manager, HR also views itself as considering longer-term issues of importance to the company, like retention and EEO. For HR a bad hire could be a recruiting and training expense or maybe even a legal hassle down the road. For the hiring manager the need is immediate, and they may feel that "bad breath is better than no breath." Both parties need to balance the short and long-term consequences by working together to enable hiring the most appropriate candidate in an expeditious manner.

Question: **What are some things HR can do to improve relations with hiring managers?**

Response: First, remember that the hiring manager is your customer. Where possible, don't rely just on a phone call to establish a good relationship with your customer. When the hiring manager calls you with a hiring need, try to meet with him/her in person, in their office as soon as they are able to see you.

Second, learn about the managers business not just his/her opening. Ask about the managers organization, its objectives, current and anticipated issues, the hiring profile and the reasons for it. Also, ask what the new hire would actually do, especially in the early period of their employment.

Third, speak to the hiring manager in business terms. Explain that you are eager to fill staffing needs, but are also mindful of the cost of a bad hire. Be realistic about your time frame to complete the hiring process without making excuses.

Question: **Is there anything HR can do to alleviate some of the time pressure hiring managers confront?**

Response: Absolutely. Make a proactive outreach to managers in anticipation of their hiring needs. For example, let's say in your company's fiscal year starts in January. Visit your potential hiring managers in the 3rd quarter and say something like this: "Last year you hired twenty new engineers. If we assume that your hiring needs will remain about the same, then let's think what we can do now to have those people on board when you need them. Let's approach your senior management together and ask for an up-front commitment to recruit and have the right people ready to go when you need them."

For another example, in a sales organization, a certain percentage of turnover is predictable. Meet with the sales managers and say, "Let's build some bench strength and schedule a training class so these new hires will be ready to go when you need them." Don't leave a sales territory open or you will jeopardize revenue opportunities.

Question: **Are there some seemingly good ideas that just don't work?**

Response: Of course, even with the best of intentions. For example, once we had an eager person in HR who developed a three-day training program to help hiring managers develop confidence in their interviewing skills. It was a conceptually and technically wonderful program in content. The problem was that none of the managers had three hours, let alone three days to devote to interviewing skills. Remember, your client, the hiring manager, has priorities that may not match yours. If you understand the boundaries up front you can develop a much better program. Another way to look at this is if your idea isn't good for your customer, it really isn't a good idea.

LESSON: You can close perceptual gaps and minimize friction if you remember that the hiring manager is your customer.

8

TRANSITION

So far, we have discussed hiring up to the point where job offers are made and accepted. Many times a hire turns out well, or turns sour, based on how the transition to the new work place is handled. This chapter contains several unfortunate mistakes to avoid.

Mistake 98: Unclear expectations

Even experienced hires may be unclear about performance expectations, as this story about Walter relates.

Walter, an experienced sales representative, was hired by Newco and set to work immediately on achieving his annual objectives. Three months later, Walter was called into his manager's office and told that he needed to work harder to achieve his benchmarks.

It turned out that Walter assumed that Newco was like Formerco and didn't expect concrete sales achievements for at least six months. Therefore, Walter focused on long term, rather than immediate results. Although this misunderstanding wasn't catastrophic, it did compel Walter to alter his selling strategy in a way that made him feel uncomfortable.

LESSON: Newco reviewed its procedures to make sure that its approach to performance and the time line for measuring it were communicated clearly throughout the interview process and during the new hire's first months with the company.

Mistake 99: Not anticipating possible rough spots

One way to increase the probability that a hire will prove to be a good one is to be prepared for specific rough spots the new employee might experience.

Monette was hired because of her skills, industry experience and upbeat personality. Her new manager and HR recognized a potential difficulty: Monette's experience was in highly structured companies and Thisco had a decidedly unstructured operating style. The manager didn't want to lose her and decided to take a chance on hiring Monette, but only after planning a support system. He put in place several down-to-earth mentors whoin Monette could turn to as she learned to operate effectively in a new environment. "We're unstructured but we couldn't let that become sink or swim," the manager noted.

LESSON: By recognizing a potential problem and putting resources in place to deal with it, Thisco didn't have to pass-up on an otherwise good candidate.

Mistake 100: Mentors are not in place

A new hire often benefits from having someone available to discuss sensitive or unclear issues. For example, when Marlene started at Certainco, she was somewhat perplexed by her manager's operating style. Unfortunately, there was nobody readily available as a confidential resource to help her clarify her quandaries. Fearing that asking too many questions of her manager would start her off on the wrong foot, Marlene stumbled through her first six weeks before being invited to discuss matters with her manager.

LESSON: New employees should have should have a "safe" or "neutral" person to speak with about problems with managers or more veteran colleagues. All new employees should be *invited* to speak with this resource *as a matter of course* in order to allay fears of appearing negative about their new employer.

Management Professor Fred Tesch (teschf@wscu.edu) observes that many companies focus on the employer's priorities for the new employee, namely, understanding the work that is to be done. For the new employee, however, the mundane context of their new work situation is a major concern. Everyday examples include dress code in practice as well as theory; the acceptability or non-acceptability in the eyes of peers of working weekends; and the appropriate uses of going for a drink after work. "The new employee is akin to a tourist in a friendly but unfamiliar country," says Professor Tesch. "She wants to know how to take care of herself and how to behave appropriately according to the standards of the local population. The history behind the great monuments and museums is a separate matter."

One way to address these important, but difficult to raise, issues is to assign a peer to the new employee. Define the attributes of the peer (age, gender, position, education) as whatever makes the peer credible to the new employee. An additional possibility is to have a question and answer type discussion of the company's cultural standards available on an Internet.

Mistake 101: The manager isn't ready for the new employee

The new employee's enthusiasm for getting started shouldn't be wasted by a slow start. Rhonda was hired by Newco and asked to start work on July 1, the first day of the company's fiscal year. Unfortunately, her manager was on a ten-day vacation at the time, recuperating from year-end overload. It took several days after his return to meet with Rhonda for an extended period. In the meantime, she was left adrift about her new projects. Rhonda's first taste of Newco's work culture was a disillusioning one that remained with her for some time.

LESSON: Just as employees should start a new job "ready to hit the ground running," employers must be ready to spend time with new employees to get them started. Set aside defined, not-to-be cancelled periods of time for the manager to meet with the new employee.

John was also eager to put his skills to work on his first day at Newco. However, he was instructed to stop by HR "to sign some forms." In fact, the "some" was a substantial pile, including forms of a legally binding nature. This initial experience put a damper on John's spirits for several reasons:

- John thought he was joining an entrepreneurial company, but his first day as an employee was thoroughly bureaucratic.

- "If this stuff is important, why didn't they tell me about it earlier?"

- There were things John didn't really understand and there was no adequate explanation available from HR. Still, John felt compelled to sign without raising a fuss.

LESSON: Newco would have been better advised to give new employees a preview of material about policies, etc., especially those requiring the employee's signature. Further, adequate answers should have been available from HR on the spot.

At Anotherco, an Orientation Day was held twice a month. At that time the "Employee Handbook" was distributed and house rules, safety regulations, and generic employee benefits were explained.

The downside was that some employees had been working up to two weeks before Orientation Day and had already signed the "Employee Handbook." Some were in the dark about safety issues when, as new employees, they were especially vulnerable.

LESSON: New employees at Anotherco are now trained in health and safety procedures on the first day. Bimonthly group orientations then serve the purpose of addressing unresolved questions of a less-life threatening nature. Documents that require a signature are addressed prior to the first working day, or the signature is delayed until after an orientation session.

9

Seven More Mistakes Not to Make

Numerous other mistakes are made which were not covered in the previous eight chapters. In addition to our 101 mistakes, the seven in this chapter still occur in many companies. Many of these mistakes emphasize the importance of understanding human behavior and being savvy in dealing with new hires.

Mistake 102: Not training everyone who interviews

Louise was a high performing line manager who had come to Certainco three month earlier. Her insights into important issues, including human nature, were highly regarded by her colleagues.

Louise was asked to serve on an interview panel as a last minute substitute. Unfortunately, Louise had not gone through interview training and she asked an illegal question. An ugly lawsuit developed as a result.

LESSON: Make sure that *everyone* who asks an interview question is trained in the process, at least to the point of not asking illegal questions. Here are some illegal questions and how to avoid them:

You Can Ask This...	...But Not This
"What is your name?"	"What was your maiden name?"
"Are you over 18?"	"When were you born?"
"Did you graduate from high school?"	"When did you graduate from high school?"
No questions about race are allowed	"What is your race?"
"Can you perform (specific tasks)?"	"Do you have physical or mental disabilities?" "Do you have a drug or alcohol problem?" "Are you taking any prescription drugs?"
"Would you be able to meet the job's requirements to work weekends frequently?"	"Would working on weekends conflict with your religion?"
"Do you have the legal right to work in the United States?"	"What country are you a citizen of?"
"Have you ever been convicted of a felony?"	"Have you ever been arrested?"
"This job requires that you speak Spanish. Do you?"	"What language did you speak in your home when you were growing up?"

Mistake 103: Fudging on the facts

Telling the truth is both an ethical imperative and good business practice.

Amanda interviewed at Greatco. The more she heard about the job and the company, the more she became interested in working there. Greatco was equally interested in hiring Amanda. There was pressure to hire such a well-qualified person, especially since the position had been open for some time. When Amanda asked about some business difficulties Greatco had experienced, the answer seemed to imply that the problems were now in the past.

Perhaps Amanda should have pressed harder on that issue. Certainly the interviewer should have been more forthcoming. Shortly after Amanda started at Greatco, financial problems resurfaced. Instead of working on the new projects that her position called for, Amanda was tasked to damage control.

"If you would have been up front with me about this possibility, I could have handled it. Now I am furious," she told an HR person at her exit interview.

LESSON: Don't lie. Don't even fudge. Be honest about possible problems. Honesty may even encourage the candidate to accept a job if offered. If not, at least you avoid the bitterness that often results from answering questions in bad faith.

Mistake 104: Not having a clear, informative job description

Never start the hiring process unless it is clear what the job description is, a lesson Certainco learned at considerable cost. Certainco needed to hire some engineers in a hurry, having just won a potentially lucrative order from a large customer. HR was asked to start bringing in candidates right away, and it did. One of them was Meg.

Unfortunately, in its haste to hire, Certainco had not written an informative job description nor carefully defined a realistic set of specs for the job. As a consequence, Meg became leery of Certainco, as did several other candidates. The net result was the need to overcome a negative perception among the professionals who had referred acquaintances and the loss of otherwise interested and viable candidates.

LESSON: No matter what the rush, have an appropriate job description and job specs in place before starting to interview candidates.

Mistake 105: Allowing the wrong people to represent your company

We can all hope that bigotry is the exception, not the rule, in the United States, but it is important to make sure that those who represent our company are not part of the exception.

Carlton was a freshly minted mechanical engineer and was interviewing on-campus with the Thingslikethisstillhappen, Inc. The interviewer, himself an engineer, didn't shake Carlton's hand, perhaps a minor *faux pas*. However the interviewer then proceeded to ask questions about one subject only—basketball. Carlton was an engineer, not an athlete, and left completely baffled when the interview ended fifteen minutes later.

Did this odd interviewing behavior reflect a bigoted worldview? Carlton, an African-American, began to think so. Other students agreed. The company was unsuccessful in its recruiting efforts at Carlton's college for the next three years.

Bigotry is not the only way to have your company poorly represented. Interpersonal behavior is another. Mary looked professionally dressed in a woman's business outfit when she interviewed at Typical College. However, when male candidates came into the interview room, Mary took off her jacket, leaned dramatically forward and told the male candidates how much fun people had at her company.

The male candidates were thoroughly flummoxed, not seeing any legitimate connection between cleavage and career.

LESSON: Be careful who you designate to interview on behalf of your company. Even putting ethical and legal issues aside, the cost of having the wrong person represent your company may be paid for years.

Mistake 106: Forgetting that new hires need early feedback

New employees are especially in need of feedback, a fact that some companies forget. For example, Niceco found that some of its new employees were performing below expectation, especially those hired straight out of college. Interviewing the under-performers, the HR staff identified two interrelated issues. First, new employees weren't quite sure about Niceco's operating procedures. Second, the new employees weren't sure how well they were performing. This second point was especially disorienting to recent college hires, who were used to frequent feedback from their professors.

LESSON: The first step was to correct an obvious oversight. New employees were given an orientation to explain the how and why of company operations. The second step was to provide early feedback for new employees, including informal reviews periodically and a formal review after six months. A mentoring system was established so that new employees could receive frank, thorough, unofficial feedback on their performance.

Mistake 107: Cutting the interview short

Sometimes, the candidate turns out to be an obvious non-hire, but completing the interview is not really a waste of time. Take the case of Tom, who was invited to interview for a customer relations position. Very early in the interview, it became clear that Tom lacked communication skills and patience. Further, he gave the impression that he had come to the interview simply hoping to get a foot in the door to interview for a completely different position. The interviewer cut the interview short, albeit thanking Tom for his time and interest.

Tom filed a suit claiming that he hadn't been given a fair chance, since his interview lasted only twenty minutes and the standard interview was forty-five minutes. The cost in time and dollars of fighting the suit far exceeded the initial time saved by the shortened interview.

LESSON: Treat every candidate equally, including those who are obviously not a good fit. On the whole, it is better to waste 25 interview minutes than to offend someone and/or risk a legal problem.

Mistake 108: Assuming that the best and the brightest are really the best (or the brightest)

Sometimes the cost of talent can be paid in indirect ways, and companies should factor that into their considerations. For example, Wonderco prided itself in hiring only the best and the brightest. "We want high achievers" was its maxim. Pursuing that maxim, Wonderco recruited heavily at top MBA programs, unquestionably, pools of great talent.

Unfortunately, to attract these top talents, Wonderco had to pay top dollar and the best and the brightest didn't have the sense not to discuss compensation within earshot of lesser mortals. The result was dissatisfaction among other staff, who then performed less well or simply left.

To compound the problem, the best and the brightest had extremely high expectations that couldn't be met. After roiling the other staff, they tended to quit.

LESSON: Brains can be found in many places, even if less consistently than at top MBA programs. Diversifying sources, Wonderco began to recruit at good, but not great, business colleges. They were able to attract some of the best students, who were delighted with their offers and challenged by their assignments.

ABOUT THE AUTHOR

Richard Fein is the Director of Placement at the University of Massachusetts (Amherst) School of Management. A career specialist for 18 years, he is widely recognized as a leading authority on developing the core career planning and job search skills—writing effective resumes and cover letters and conducting winning job interviews. He is author of five major career books: ***100 Great Jobs and How to Get Them, 101 Dynamite Questions to Ask at Your Job Interview; 101 Quick Tips For a Dynamite Resume; 111 Dynamite Ways to Ace Your Job Interview, First Job,*** and ***Cover Letters! Cover Letters! Cover Letters!***

Richard has been a contributor to the *Wall Street Journal's Managing Your Career* and a columnist for *Employment Review Magazine.* He is a frequent commentator on the job search process for both print and electronic media. He has appeared as a guest on more than 30 radio and television programs and has been quoted in newspapers as diverse as the *Christian Science Monitor* and the *Idaho Statesman.*

Richard holds an MBA from Baruch College in New York, an MA in Political Science from the City University of New York, and a BA in Political Science from the University of Pennsylvania. He can be contacted via email through his publisher, Impact Publications, at: *rfein@impactpublications.com.*

BUSINESS AND CAREER RESOURCES

Contact Impact Publications for a free annotated listing of resources or visit the World Wide Web for a complete listing of resources: www.impactpublications.com. The following books are available directly from Impact Publications. Complete the following form or list the titles, include postage (see formula at the end), enclose payment, and send your order to:

IMPACT PUBLICATIONS
9104 Manassas Drive, Suite N
Manassas Park, VA 20111-5211
Tel 1-800/361-1055, 703/361-7300, or Fax 703/335-9486
Quick and easy online ordering: *www.impactpublications.com*

Qty.	Titles	Price	Total
BOOKS BY RICHARD FEIN			
_____	100 Great Jobs and How to Get Them	17.95	_____
_____	101 Dynamite Questions to Ask at Your Job Interview	14.95	_____
_____	101 Hiring Mistakes Employers Make...Avoid Them	14.95	_____
_____	101 Quick Tips For a Dynamite Resume	13.95	_____
_____	111 Dynamite Ways to Ace Your Job Interview	13.95	_____
_____	Cover Letters! Cover Letters! Cover Letters!	9.99	_____
_____	First Job	12.95	_____
THE CAREERSAVVY SERIES			
_____	100 Top Internet Job Sites	12.95	_____
_____	101 Hiring Mistakes Employers Make...Avoid Them	14.95	_____
_____	Anger and Conflict in the Workplace	15.95	_____
_____	The Best 100 Web Sites for HR Professionals	12.95	_____
_____	The Difficult Hire	14.95	_____
_____	Savvy Interviewing	10.95	_____
_____	The Savvy Resume Writer	12.95	_____
HIRING & RETENTION			
_____	45 Effective Ways for Hiring Smart!	24.95	_____
_____	96 Great Interview Questions to Ask Before You Hire	16.95	_____
_____	Ask the Right Questions, Hire the Best People	14.99	_____
_____	CareerXroads 2000	26.95	_____
_____	Complete Reference Checking Handbook	29.95	_____
_____	Directory of Executive Recruiters 2000	44.95	_____
_____	Employer's Guide to Recruiting on the Internet	24.95	_____
_____	Essential Book of Interviewing	15.00	_____
_____	Fast Forward MBA in Hiring	14.95	_____
_____	Finding and Keeping Great Employees	24.95	_____
_____	High Impact Hiring	34.95	_____
_____	Hire With Your Head	29.95	_____

Qty.	Titles	Price	Total
_____	Hiring: How to Find & Keep the Best People	12.99	_____
_____	Hiring and Managing Personnel Library	299.95	_____
_____	Love 'Em or Lose 'Em	17.95	_____
_____	Manager's Book of Questions	12.95	_____
_____	Smart Hiring	12.95	_____
_____	Smart Staffing	19.95	_____
_____	Unofficial Guide to Hiring & Firing Employees	16.00	_____
_____	Verify Those Credentials	19.95	_____
_____	Weddle's Guide to Employment Web-sites	21.95	_____

MOTIVATING & ENERGIZING YOUR WORKFORCE

Qty.	Titles	Price	Total
_____	1001 Ways to Energize Employees	12.00	_____
_____	1001 Ways to Reward Employees	12.00	_____
_____	Bringing Out the Best in People	21.95	_____
_____	Dilbert Principle	20.00	_____
_____	Getting Employees to Fall in Love with Your Company	17.95	_____
_____	How to Be a Star at Work	12.00	_____
_____	Joy of Work	22.00	_____
_____	Motivating and Rewarding Employees	99.00	_____
_____	Motivation and Goal-Setting	99.00	_____
_____	Passionate Organization	24.95	_____
_____	Take This Job and Thrive	14.95	_____

RESUMES & LETTERS

Qty.	Titles	Price	Total
_____	100 Winning Resumes for $100,000+ Jobs	24.95	_____
_____	101 Quick Tips for a Dynamite Resume	13.95	_____
_____	201 Winning Cover Letters for the $100,000+ Jobs	24.95	_____
_____	1500+ Key Words for 100,000+	14.95	_____
_____	Dynamite Cover Letters	14.95	_____
_____	Dynamite Resumes	14.95	_____
_____	Haldane's Best Cover Letters for Professionals	15.95	_____
_____	Haldane's Best Resumes for Professionals	15.95	_____
_____	High Impact Resumes and Letters	19.95	_____
_____	Sure-Hire Resumes	14.95	_____
_____	Winning Resumes	10.95	_____

INTERVIEWING: JOBSEEKERS

Qty.	Titles	Price	Total
_____	101 Dynamite Answers to Interview Questions	12.95	_____
_____	101 Dynamite Questions to Ask at Your Job Interview	14.95	_____
_____	101 Tough Interview Questions. . .	14.95	_____
_____	111 Dynamite Ways to Ace Your Job Interview	13.95	_____
_____	Haldane's Best Answers to Tough Interview Questions	15.95	_____
_____	Interview for Success	15.95	_____
_____	Savvy Interviewing	10.95	_____

NETWORKING AND THE INTERNET

Qty.	Titles	Price	Total
_____	100 Top Internet Job Sites	12.95	_____
_____	Dynamite Networking for Dynamite Jobs	15.95	_____
_____	Dynamite Tele-Search	12.95	_____
_____	Electronic Resumes	19.95	_____
_____	Internet Resumes	14.95	_____

SALARY NEGOTIATIONS

Qty.	Titles	Price	Total
_____	Dynamite Salary Negotiations	15.95	_____
_____	Get a Raise in 7 Days	14.95	_____

Qty.	Titles	Price	Total
_____	Get More Money on Your Next Job	14.95	_____
_____	Negotiate Your Job Offer	14.95	_____

IMAGE, ETIQUETTE, & COMMUNICATION

Qty.	Titles	Price	Total
_____	101 Secrets of Highly Effective Speakers	14.95	_____
_____	Dressing Smart in the New Millennium	15.95	_____
_____	John Malloy's Dress for Success (For Men)	13.99	_____
_____	New Women's Dress for Success	12.99	_____
_____	Red Socks Don't Work	14.95	_____
_____	You've Only Got 3 Seconds	22.95	_____

JOB STRATEGIES AND TACTICS

Qty.	Titles	Price	Total
_____	101 Ways to Power Up Your Job Search	12.95	_____
_____	110 Big Mistakes Job Hunters Make	19.95	_____
_____	24 Hours to Your Next Job, Raise, or Promotion	10.95	_____
_____	Better Book for Getting Hired	11.95	_____
_____	Career Bounce-Back	14.95	_____
_____	Career Chase	17.95	_____
_____	Career Fitness	19.95	_____
_____	Career Intelligence	15.95	_____
_____	Career Starter	10.95	_____
_____	Coming Alive From 9 to 5	18.95	_____
_____	Complete Idiot's Guide to Changing Careers	17.95	_____
_____	Executive Job Search Strategies	16.95	_____
_____	First Job Hunt Survival Guide	11.95	_____
_____	Five Secrets to Finding a Job	12.95	_____
_____	Get a Job You Love!	19.95	_____
_____	Get It Together By 30	14.95	_____
_____	Get the Job You Want Series	37.95	_____
_____	Get Ahead! Stay Ahead!	12.95	_____
_____	Getting from Fired to Hired	14.95	_____
_____	Great Jobs for Liberal Arts Majors	11.95	_____
_____	How to Get a Job in 90 Days or Less	12.95	_____
_____	How to Get Interviews from Classified Job Ads	14.95	_____
_____	How to Succeed Without a Career Path	13.95	_____
_____	How to Make Use of a Useless Degree	13.00	_____
_____	Is It Too Late To Run Away and Join the Circus?	14.95	_____
_____	Job Hunting in the 21st Century	17.95	_____
_____	Job Hunting for the Utterly Confused	14.95	_____
_____	Job Hunting Made Easy	12.95	_____
_____	Job Search: The Total System	14.95	_____
_____	Job Search Organizer	12.95	_____
_____	Job Search Time Manager	14.95	_____
_____	JobShift	13.00	_____
_____	JobSmart	12.00	_____
_____	Kiplinger's Survive and Profit From a Mid-Career Change	12.95	_____
_____	Knock 'Em Dead	12.95	_____
_____	Me, Myself, and I, Inc.	17.95	_____
_____	New Rights of Passage	29.95	_____
_____	No One Is Unemployable	29.95	_____
_____	Not Just Another Job	12.00	_____
_____	Perfect Job Search	12.95	_____
_____	Princeton Review Guide to Your Career	20.00	_____
_____	Perfect Pitch	13.99	_____
_____	Portable Executive	12.00	_____
_____	Professional's Job Finder	18.95	_____
_____	Right Fit	14.95	_____
_____	Right Place at the Right Time	11.95	_____
_____	Second Careers	14.95	_____

Qty.	Titles	Price	Total
_____	Secrets from the Search Firm Files	24.95	_____
_____	So What If I'm 50	12.95	_____
_____	Staying in Demand	12.95	_____
_____	Strategic Job Jumping	13.00	_____
_____	SuccessAbilities	14.95	_____
_____	Take Yourself to the Top	13.99	_____
_____	Temping: The Insiders Guide	14.95	_____
_____	Top 10 Career Strategies for the Year 2000 & Beyond	12.00	_____
_____	Top 10 Fears of Job Seekers	12.00	_____
_____	Ultimate Job Search Survival	14.95	_____
_____	Welcome to the Real World	13.00	_____
_____	What Do I Say Next?	20.00	_____
_____	What Employers Really Want	14.95	_____
_____	When Do I Start	11.95	_____
_____	Who Says There Are No Jobs Out There	12.95	_____
_____	Work Happy Live Healthy	14.95	_____
_____	Work This Way	14.95	_____

INSPIRATION & EMPOWERMENT

Qty.	Titles	Price	Total
_____	Beating Job Burnout	12.95	_____
_____	Chicken Soup for the Soul Series	87.95	_____
_____	Do What You Love, the Money Will Follow	11.95	_____
_____	Get What You Deserve	23.00	_____
_____	If Life Is A Game, These Are the Rules	15.00	_____
_____	Seven Habits of Highly Effective People	14.00	_____

☞ **SUBTOTAL** $ _____

☞ Virginia residents add 4½% sales tax)   _____

☞ Shipping/handling, Continental U.S., $5.00 +   _____ $5.00
plus following percentages when **SUBTOTAL** is:

   ☐ $30-$100—multiply SUBTOTAL by 8%   _____

   ☐ $100-$999—multiply SUBTOTAL by 7%   _____

   ☐ $1,000-$4,999—multiply SUBTOTAL by 6%   _____

   ☐ Over $5,000—multiply SUBTOTAL by 5%   _____

☞ ☐ If shipped outside Continental US, add another 5%   _____

☞ **TOTAL ENCLOSED** $_____

SHIP TO: (street address only for UPS or RPS delivery)

Name _____

Address _____

_____

_____

Telephone _____

I enclose ☐ Check ☐ Money Order in the amount of: $ _____

Charge $_____ to ☐ Visa ☐ MC ☐ AmEx

Card # _____ Exp: _____ / _____

Signature _____

DISCOVER HUNDREDS OF ADDITIONAL RESOURCES ON THE WORLD WIDE WEB!

Looking for the newest and best books, directories, newsletters, wall charts, training programs, videos, computer software, and kits to help you energize your employees, effectively address sexual harassment issues, or improve your networking skills? Want to learn the most effective way to find a job in Asia or relocate to San Francisco? Are you curious about how to recruit a new employee using the Internet or about what you'll be doing five years from now? Are you trying to keep up-to-date on the latest HR resources, but are not able to find the latest catalogs, brochures, or newsletters on today's "best of the best" resources?

Welcome to the first virtual career bookstore on the Internet. Now you're only a click away with Impact Publications' electronic solution to the resource challenge. Visit this rich site to quickly discover everything you ever wanted to know about workplace diversity, career development, and compensation and benefits—including many useful resources that are difficult to find in local bookstores and libraries. The site also includes what's new and hot, tips for job search success, and monthly specials. Check it out today!

www.impactpublications.com

Don't be kept in the dark... Sign Up For Impact's *FREE* E-Zine Today!

Get the latest information and special discounts on career, business, and travel products through our new electronic magazine (e-zine). Becoming a member of this exclusive "What's New and Special" group is quick and easy. Just enter your email address online on our Web site:

www.impactpublications.com

Or, email your email address to joinlist@impactpublications.com, or fax it to (703/335-9486).

Impact Publications ◆ 9104 Manassas Drive, Suite N ◆ Manassas Park, VA 20111-5211 ◆ 703/361-7300 ◆ www.impactpublications.com